Introduction

Because of the fallen nature of mankind, everyone is being born a sinner and into different kinds of battles. The battles may vary from one individual to the other, but the fact is that; no one escapes the battles of this life. All of life's battles are being pioneered by Satan and his demons against the souls of men and women. Only those that believe in Jesus Christ and are truly born again can receive God's Holy Spirit which empowers and helps a person to overcome the battles targeting his or her soul. There is no way one can be a true Christian, do the will of God, or please God, without the Holy Spirit being present in his or her life. In this battle for the soul, the ignorant folks perish in the same way as those that ignore the battle.

God is a warrior and therefore requires that all of His children be likewise. The devil is God's enemy, and therefore, the devil is the enemy of the entire human race. You do not have to offend the Satan for him to hate you; Satan had already hated you before you were born in this world. Being a born again and living a Holy life gives you an edge over the battles of life and a green light of God's support to you through the finished work of Jesus Christ on cavalry's cross. As believers, when we know God's word, we will know our authority in Christ Jesus. As we put our faith in God and obey God's words, we'll not only get the victory over life's battles, but we will wax even stronger and do exploit things.

A Christian should be wise enough to know the tricks of the devil if the Christian is to be victorious in the battles of this life. As warriors, being aware of the front we are warring from makes the battle even easier. Warfare prayers are what the devil and his demons understand nowadays, there is no room for ceremonial prayers.

Since the battles we face in this life are been pioneered by the forces of darkness, victory can only be obtained when those evil powers have been seriously dealt with. If the evil forces pioneering battles against a person's life are not thoroughly dealt with, true success can be difficult for that person. This might also cost a person eternal life.

Acknowledgement: My special thanks and appreciation goes to the HOLY SPIRIT of GOD for giving me His immeasurable inspiration, grace and strength in the writing of this book which is to the Glory of JESUS CHRIST, Son of the living GOD. Unto Him belongs all the Glory forever. Amen.

Note: *all scriptures from KJV, except order wise stated.*

Contents

Chapter 1

Everything in this life is a Battle.

Have you ever given a good thought about the world we are living in? If you have, you must have noticed that in every stage of our lives on this earth, we are faced with situations and circumstances that appear to be challenging. Every aspect of this life we are living is a battle. This might not appear to be clear to you, but it is the truth about this life we are living. From childhood through adulthood to old age, every step in this life brings new challenges that we must overcome.

Job, in the Bible said, *"Man is born unto trouble." Job 5:7*. Job was a man that did not only serve God, but his relationship with God in his days was unique. *Job 1:8 "And the Lord said unto Satan, hast thou considered my servant Job, that there is none like him in the earth, a perfect and an upright man, one that feared God, and eschewed evil?"* But despite the good relationship Job had with God, Job faced a lot of troubles in his days.

The word "Battle" in every sense is referring to some kind of a fight. You being a Christian or not, it does not matter; the battle is still going on. Whether you know of the battle or not, it does not matter; the battle is still going on. Whether you want to fight or not, it does no matter; the battle is still going on. Whether you approve of this battle or not, the enemy will still fight you. *"THIS IS A BATTLE FOR YOUR SOUL."*

You are a spirit, having a soul, and living in a body. *Genesis 2:7 "And the Lord God formed man of the dust of the ground, and breathed into his nostrils the breath of life; and man became a living soul". Also in 1 Thessalonians 5:23 "And the very God of peace sanctify you wholly; and I pray God your whole spirit and soul and body be preserved blameless unto the coming of our Lord Jesus Christ". And in Ecclesiastes 12:7 "Then shall the dust return to the earth as it was: and the spirit shall return unto God who gave it".* In these verses we just read, the Holy Scriptures confirmed to us that; man is a spirit, having a soul, and living in a body.

The Bible revealed to us that God our creator is a spirit. *John 4:24 "God is a Spirit: and they that worship Him must worship Him in spirit and in truth".* And then in *Genesis 1:26 "And God said, let us make man in our image, after our likeness: and let them have dominion over the fish of the sea and over the fowl of the air, and over the cattle, and over all the earth, and over every creeping thing that crept upon the earth".* Meaning, since God, who created man is a spirit, and God said He created us in His own image, then, we are spirit beings like God. The breath of life that God breathed into the nostrils of Adam was the breath of God's spirit. This is the reason why every human being must breathe in and out to live. But this breath is absolutely God's own property. This makes abortion a sin, and it is wrong to destroy any human life. That's why God said in *Ecclesiastes 12:7 "Then shall the dust return to the earth as it was: and the spirit shall return unto God who gave it"*. Therefore, whether you are a Christian or not, God will one day take back the breath He breathed into your nostrils, because it is God's property. So know that; this life you are living is not yours. God just gave it to you for a short period; testing you to see if you will prove to be grateful, faithful, sincere, honest and obedient to God. *1 Corinthians 4:2 "Moreover it is required in stewards that a man is found faithful"*. We are stewards, so we must be careful to live in accordance with God's will and purpose, because the person that does not prove to be honest and faithful in this life will not receive eternal life. *Luke 16:11 "If therefore ye have not been faithful in the unrighteous mammon, who will commit to your trust the true riches?"*

The soul is God's image in man. God will only accept back to Himself the image He placed in you if the image is not being contaminated with sin. On the Day of Judgment, the soul will give witness before God and give account of all it has been involved in whiles on this earth. *Romans 12:14 "So then every one of us shall give account of himself to God"*. The responsibility of keeping your Soul from being contaminated by sin is entirely yours and it is only possible when you surrender your life to Jesus Christ. Satan the devil is doing all he can to contaminate the soul of a person, so God can punish that person together with him; here then comes the battle.

From the day a child is conceived in the mother's womb, the devil starts to fight that soul. *2 Thessalonians 2:4 "Who opposed and exalted himself above all that is called God, or that is worshipped; so that he as god sixtieth in the temple of God, showing himself that he is God"*. This verse makes us to know that, from the moment God kicked Lucifer from heaven, Lucifer, has to this day been and will ever remain God's enemy. Satan knows he will never receive pardon from God for the rebellion he started in heaven, because God will not change. *Malachi 3:6a "For I am the Lord, I change not"*. The judgment of God has been set and nothing can change it. *Mathew 25:41 "Then shall He say also unto them on the left hand, depart from me, ye cursed, into everlasting fire, prepared for the devil and his angels"*. God made hell for Satan and his demons (those angels that followed Satan in his rebellion against God). God did not make hell fire for human beings.

God made us to be like Himself, because God loves us. Satan was in heaven and has seen and experienced God's power. Satan knows that God's authority is final in all creation. *1 chronicles 17:20 "O Lord, there is none like thee, neither is there any God beside thee, according to all that we have heard with our ears"*. God created all the angels including Lucifer, to serve Him, but Lucifer who later became known as Satan or the devil, rebelled and led a rebellion against God in heaven.

The devil fully knows that God's judgment awaits him and that God will punish him with all his demons. Therefore, the devil is trying to make every human being to be full of sin like he is. The devil fully knows that God is holy, and that God will punish sin of any kind. God is so holy that His eyes cannot look at sin. *1 Peter1:16 "Because it is written: be ye holy, for 1 am holy. To be holy is to be without sin. The opposite of holiness is sinfulness, and God will punish every sin. Proverbs 11:21$_a$ "Though hands join in hand, the wicked shall not be unpunished"*. Also in *Nahum 1:3$_{a-b}$ "The Lord is slow to anger, and great in power, and will not at all acquit the wicked"*. God will never let an un-repented sin of any kind go unpunished. All the devil is trying to do is to make a person to sin against God and look like him, so mankind can share in his punishment. That is why:

1. **You have to fight for your Soul**. *Luke 21:19 "In your patience possess ye your souls"*. Why did our Lord Jesus Christ make this statement, meditate on these words of our Lord Jesus Christ; *"In your patience possess ye your souls"*. In your "patience" (continuous battle for your soul through the redemption power in the blood of Jesus) you will possess your soul. *Colossians 1:14 "In whom we have redemption through His blood, even the forgiveness of sins"*. This verse clearly shows that we can only be redeemed from sin and death through the cleansing power in the precious blood of Jesus Christ.

2. **You have to fight against sin of any kind**. *Hebrews 12:4 "Ye have not yet resisted unto blood, striving against sin"*. In this verse, note the word "striving" which means "struggling, fighting". Our striving against sin should be forceful. If you are striving against sin without been forceful, it is the same as compromising with sin. *Isaiah 9:5 "For every battle of the warrior is with confused noise, and garments rolled in blood; but this shall be with burning and fuel of fire"*. Christians are called to be warriors, why? It is because God our creator is a warrior. You might hate sin, but if you do not strive against it forcefully, it will eventually overcome you in the end. Remember it is "sin" you are "striving" against, not the "sinner" (the individual committing the sin). God hates sin, but not the sinner. Also in *2 Timothy 2:19 "Nevertheless the foundation of God standout sure having this seal, the Lord knoweth*

them that are His, and let everyone that nameth the name of Christ depart from iniquity". 1Thessalonians 5:22 "abstain from all appearance of evil". Do not be a hypocrite, you cannot trick God. *Galatians 6:7 "Be not deceived; God is not mocked: for whatsoever a man soweth, that shall he also reap".*

The devil knows that in order for him to get the soul of a man, he will have to fight that man in every area of his life continually. This is the reason why humanity is experiencing all these miss apps in the world today. Unborn children are targeted through abortion, not to talk of us living now. The devil is fighting humanity in every aspect; in our relationship with God, in our health, in our families, in our marriages, in our homes, in our schools, in our work places, in our businesses, in our dreams, in our finances, in our relationships with others, in our daily lives, on our streets, against our destinies, against our peace, against our joy, against our happiness, against our progress, against our success, against our prosperity, against our greatness, against our love for God, against our love for others, against our unity, against our friendships, against our kindness, against our service to God, against our obedience to God.

In every area of your life and at every moment of your life, the devil hates you with the strongest of passion. *2 Thessalonians 2:4$_a$ "Who opposeth and exalteth himself above all that is called God, or that is worshipped".* The devil hates you because you were created by God and in the image of God. So for you to have true success in any area of your life, you must battle. Battle for your soul, battle for your life, battle for your health, battle for your destiny, battle for your family, battle for your marriage, battle for your children, battle for your home, battle for your peace, battle for your joy, battle for your happiness, battle for your success, battle for your progress, battle for your finances, and battle for your possessions.

You have to battle in prayer for everything. Satan hates God and everything that God has created. So do not befriend Satan, "Satan is your enemy". Join forces with God today, and defeat your enemy the devil. *James 4:7-8 "$_7$submit yourselves therefore to God, resist the devil and he will flee from you. $_8$Draw nigh to God, and He will draw nigh to you. Cleanse your hands, ye sinners, and purify your hearts, ye double minded".* Remember, with God, our victory is sure. *Romans 8:31 "What shall we then say to these things? If God be for us, who can be against us?". 1 Corinthians15:57 "But thanks be to God, which giveth us the victory through our Lord Jesus Christ".*

Chapter 2

Stop being Ignorant.

Most Christians do not know the kind of life God has called them into. Being ignorant of the battle you are in will not exclude you from the attacks of your enemy. God said in His word, *Hosea 4:6 "My people are destroyed for lack of knowledge: because thou hast rejected knowledge, I will also reject thee, that thou shalt be no priest to me: seeing thou hast forgotten the law of thy God, I will also forget thy children"*. The "lack of knowledge," God is talking about here is; ignorance. If you have decided to serve God, then you must be ready to march with God as He goes into battle against His enemies.

God is looking for militant Christians that can take the battle to the gates of the enemy; King David was that type of a Christian. King David did not only deliver the nation of Israel from the treats of Goliath, but he was also a spiritual warrior God depended on. In *psalms 24:7-10 "Lift up your heads, O ye gates; and be ye lift up, ye everlasting doors; and the King of Glory shall come in. ₈Who is this King of Glory? The Lord strong and mighty, the Lord mighty in battle. ₉Lift up your heads, O ye gates; even lift them up, ye everlasting doors; and the King of Glory shall come in. ₁₀Who is this King of glory? The Lord of hosts, He is the King of Glory"*. This prayer of King David was both a prophecy and a warfare prayer. King David was actually given a command to the hosts of hell to bow unto the Lordship of Jesus Christ. Immediately after His death on the cross, our Lord Jesus Christ went down to hell to preach to the spirits that were in prison. *1 peter 3:19 "By which also He went and preached unto the spirits in prison"*. King David said this prayer over 800 years before our Lord Jesus Christ was born. God is looking for men and women that will take the battle to the gates of His enemies. God is not looking for people that will be a liability to His kingdom. *Matthew 23:13 "But woe unto you, scribes and Pharisees, hypocrites, for ye shut up the kingdom of heaven against men: for ye neither go in yourselves, neither suffer ye them that are entering to go in"*. Do not be that kind of a Christian.

With all the experiences of war he had, King Saul never had the nerve to face Goliath. God had to use David, a poor shepherd boy, who stood his ground against the giant-Goliath and killed him. If Saul, king (president) of Israel, could not deliver the nation of Israel from a single giant that was defying the armies of Israel. *1 Samuel 17:10-11 "And the Philistine said, I defy the armies of Israel this day; give me a man, that we may fight together. ₁₁When Saul and all Israel heard those words of the Philistine, they were dismayed, and greatly afraid".* Since Saul, king of Israel failed in his duty to stand against Goliath and defend the nation of Israel, Saul's presence on Israel's throne was no longer necessary.

Your mandate as a Christian is to destroy the works of darkness, and establish righteousness. *Jeremiah 1:10 "See, I have this day set thee over the nations and over the kingdoms, to root out, and to pull down, and to destroy, and to throw down, to build, and to plant".* The Church is meant to be a military barracks, not a company of civilians. *Luke 4:18 "The Spirit of the Lord is upon me, because He hath anointed me to preach the gospel to the poor; He hath sent me to heal the brokenhearted, to preach deliverance to the captives, and recovering of sight to the blind, to set at liberty them that are bruised".*

Ephesians 6:12-17 "For we wrestle not against flesh and blood, but against principalities, against powers, against the rulers of the darkness of this world, against spiritual wickedness in high places. ₁₃Wherefore take unto you the whole armor of God that ye may be able to withstand in the evil day, and having done all, to stand. ₁₄Stand therefore, having your loins girt about with truth, and having on the breastplate of righteousness. ₁₅and your feet shod with the preparation of the gospel of peace. ₁₆Above all, taking the shield of faith, wherewith ye shall be able to quench all the fiery darts of the wicked.₁₇And take the helmet of salvation, and the sword of the Spirit, which is the word of God". This scripture tells us clearly that: 1. We are in a war. 2. The war we are in is spiritual. 3. We must fight in other to be able to stand or overcome. Verses13-17 tells of the armor of God, a complete set of military dress.

A warrior ready for battle.

You must fight to get the victory, or you will be the victim. *Jeremiah 48:10* *"Cursed be he that doeth the work of the Lord deceitfully, and cursed be he that keepeth back his sword from blood".*

Chapter 3

God, our creator is a warrior.

From creation until now, God has always proven to be a warrior fighting against His enemies. The Bible makes it very clear that; God is against evil and all those that do the devil's biddings. *Exodus 15:3 "The Lord is a man of war; the Lord is His name".* From Genesis to Revelation, God has made it clear to humanity that He is against every form of iniquity, wrong doing, and sin of any kind. God hates wickedness to the core and will punish every form of wickedness.

The Bible makes it clear to us that; Satan is God's enemy. *Isaiah 14:12-15 "How art thou fallen from heaven, O Lucifer, son of the morning! How art thou cut down to the ground, which didst weaken the nations! 13For thou hast said in thine heart, I will ascend into heaven, I will exalt my throne above the stars of God; I will sit also upon the mount of the congregation, in the sides of the north. 14 I will ascend above the heights of the clouds; I will be like the most High. 15Yet thou shalt be brought down to hell, to the sides of the pit".* Since the day God kicked Satan out of heaven, Satan has not seized to be an enemy to God. When God created Adam and Eve, the devil saw it as an opportunity to fight back against God by misleading Adam and his wife, causing them to sin against God. The devil clearly knows that he has lost his opportunity and place in heaven, and that is the reason why the devil doesn't want you to enter heaven. If you have given your life to Jesus Christ, make no mistake about it. Because by giving your life to Jesus Christ, it means you have Joined alliance with God in the fight against His enemies. *Matthew 12:30 "He that is not with me is against me; and he that gathereth not with me scattereth abroad".*

The devil knows that, sin in every form irritates God so much. *Psalms 5:5-6 "For thou art not a God that hath pleasure in wickedness, neither shall evil dwell with thee. 6the foolish shall not stand in thy sight; thou hatest all workers of iniquity".* The devil also knows that God loves mankind so much. *John 3:16 "For God so loved the world that He gave His only begotten son, that whosoever believeth in Him should not perish, but have everlasting life".* If God never loved mankind, God would not have sent His son Jesus Christ to die on the cross for the sins of mankind.

Even when God sent His son Jesus Christ to die for the sins of man, the devil and his allies joined together in order to hinder God's plan of salvation for mankind. *Psalms 2:1-2 "Why do the heathen rage, and the people imagine a vain thing? 2The kings of the earth set themselves, and the rulers take counsel together against the Lord and against His anointed".* When Jesus was born, King Herod sought to kill him. By that, King Herod ended up killing a great number of innocent children. *Matthew 2:16 "Then Herod, when he saw that he was mocked of the wise men, was exceeding wroth, and sent forth, and slew all the children that were in Bethlehem, and in all the coasts thereof, from two years old and under, according to the time which he had diligently inquired of the wise men".*

This battle will only end on the day God gives His final judgment against the devil and all the workers of iniquity. *Matthew 25:31-34, 41 "When the Son of man shall come in His glory and all the holy angels with Him, then shall He sit upon the throne of His glory. ₃₂And before Him shall be gathered all nations and He shall separate them one from another, as a shepherd divideth his sheep from the goats. ₃₃And He shall set the sheep on His right hand, but the goats on the left. ₃₄Then shall the King say unto them on His right hand, Come, ye blessed of my Father, inherit the kingdom prepared for you from the foundation of the world. ₄₁Then shall He say also unto them on the left hand, depart from me, ye cursed, into everlasting fire, prepared for the devil and his angels".*

It has always been God's desire that every believer should come to the understanding that Christianity is not just any kind of religion. From creation until now, the devil has tried all he can to hinder the kingdom of God. From the day God appeared to Abraham and established His covenant with him, the devil immediately started fighting against Abraham and his seed. Moses knew that God does have enemies, therefore he prayed in *Numbers 10:35 "And it came to pass, when the ark set forward, that Moses said, rise up, Lord, and let thine enemies be scattered; and let them that hate thee flee before thee".* King David also knew very well that God does have enemies. *Psalm 68:1 "Let God arise; let His enemies be scattered, let them also that hate Him flee before Him".* The apostle Paul also knew very well that God does have enemies. If your Christianity is to be of any worth to the kingdom of heaven, then you must know that God is a warrior and He does have enemies. *2 Thessalonians 2:4 "Who opposeth and exalteth himself above all that is called God or that is worshipped".*

Most Christians have been victims to the devil today because they don't know what God has called them into. Being ignorant of you being in a war will not prevent you from being shot at by your enemies. God is looking for warriors, men and women who are spiritually violent enough to harass the devil and his demons and take the battle to the gates of hell. *Matthew 11:12 "And from the days of John the Baptist until now, the kingdom of heaven suffereth violence, and the violent take it by force".* Only the spiritually violent Christians will take back their portion from the grip of the enemy. *Luke 10:19 "Behold, I give unto you power to tread on serpents and scorpions, and over all the power of the enemy, and nothing shall by any means hurt you".* Christians should be trampling over the devil and his cohorts. Christians should not be complaining and running from one pointed to the other because they are fearful of the attacks of the devil. With a single Christian in any environment, the forces of darkness should not carry out their operations in that environment. But the opposite is what exactly we are seeing today. Christians are very much likely to run away from good things because they are afraid of the enemy. A pastor from a prayer-based church was employed in a certain office with a very good pay. As the pastor sat in his office one day, an image appeared in the office. Within the next two days, pastor resigned his job. With all the power in the word of God, the pastor could not stand a mere intimidation from the kingdom of darkness. Because of his cowardice, pastor loosed is hard found job.

Chapter 4

Who is my enemy?

Make no mistake about this; because you were created by God, "the devil is your enemy and the devil will fight against you". This is not an issue of whether you have a relationship with Jesus Christ or not. Whether you have a relationship with Jesus Christ or not, the devil will fight you. The goal of the devil is to reap off your soul from the eternal connection you have with God.

God created man in His own very image. *Genesis 1:26-27 "And God said, let us make man in our image, after our likeness: and let them have dominion over the fish of the sea and over the fowl of the air, and over the cattle, and over all the earth, and over every creeping thing that creepeth upon the earth. ₂₇So God created man in His own image, in the image of God created He him; male and female created He them".* God made human beings to look like Him; in His own image God created us. Do not think you are of no importance to God because things are not working for you the way you expected. Of all that God created in this entire universe, you are the most important of all, because you were made in God's own very image; the image of God. Of all God's creation, there is none to give an account or to face judgment but mankind, because mankind was created in the very image of God. Since the devil knows he cannot fight against God and win, the devil is therefore fighting against mankind that God created in His own very image; the image of God. *2 Thessalonians 2:4ₐ "Who opposeth and exalteth himself above all that is called God, or that is worshipped".* The devil opposes everything that God has created and everything that God has put in place, simply because the devil is against God and everything that belongs to God. *Revelation 12:17 "And the dragon was wroth with the woman: and went to make war with the remnant of her seed which keep the commandments of God, and have the testimony of Jesus Christ".* This scripture in Revelation 12:17 revealed to us that the devil is making war with the remnants of the seed of the woman. That refers to me and you that are presently living on this earth; we are the seed of the woman.

When the devil caused Adam and Eve to sin against God in the Garden of Eden, God told the devil that He will put enmity between the woman and the devil, and between the seed of the woman and the seed of the devil. The seed of the devil are the demonic personalities, but then, anyone that is involved in sin of any kind or form is doing the works of the devil, and therefore belongs to the devil. *1 John 3:8-10 "he that committeth sin is of the devil; for the devil sinneth from the beginning. For this purpose the Son of God was manifested, that He might destroy the works of the devil. ₉Whosoever is born of God doth not commit sin; for His seed remaineth in him: and he cannot sin, because he is born of God. ₁₀In this the children of God are manifest, and the children of the devil: whosoever doeth not righteousness is not of God, neither he that loveth not his brother"*. Here a clear distinction is set, an absolute way of differentiating between the children of God and the children of the devil. So regardless of whether a man is serving God or not, that man is a direct enemy to the devil because that man was created in the very image of God and by God. Even those individuals involved in sin still remains to be an enemy to the devil, regardless of the extent to which they are serving or doing the works of the devil. *John 10:10 "The thief cometh not, but for to steal, and to kill, and to destroy: I am come that they might have life and that they might have it more abundantly"*. Satan is a deceiver; do not let Satan deceive you.

Make no mistake about it, if you are serving and living for God in righteousness, purity and true holiness; God knows you. *2 Timothy 2:19 "Nevertheless the foundation of God standeth sure, having this seal; the Lord knoweth them that are His. And let everyone that nameth the name of Christ depart from iniquity"*. God knows those that truly belong to Him and has therefore sealed them with His Holy Spirit. *2 Corinthians 1:22 "Who hath also sealed us: and given the earnest of the Spirit in our hearts"*. This verse clearly tells us that God has sealed every true believer with His Holy Spirit as a guarantee of God's salvation. This verse also indicates that, any Christian that does not have the spirit of God in him does not belong to God and does not have eternal life. *Romans 8:9 "But ye are not in the flesh, but in the Spirit; if so be that the Spirit of God dwell in you; now if any man have not the Spirit of Christ, he is none of His"*.

Most times we are faced with situations that make us see other people around us to be our enemies, and most times we do refer to them as enemies because of what they might have done to us. Most Christians are found wanting of this; referring to other people as their enemies because of what might have transpired between them. That is not right. The entire human race is just a family of brothers and sisters. All humanity descended from the same ancestors (Adam and Eve) regardless of color, race, language, and background. We are all the same people created equally by God. *1 John 3:15 "Whosoever hateth his brother is a murderer and ye know that no murderer hath eternal life abiding in him"*. This verse makes it clear to us that;

discrimination is a sin. Mankind's only enemy is Satan the devil and the demonic personalities working with Satan. You must not forget this; "the battle we are in is not physical, but spiritual". *Ephesians 6:12 "For we wrestle not against flesh and blood, but against principalities, against powers, against the rulers of the darkness of this world, against spiritual wickedness in high places".* Also *2 Corinthians 10:3-4 "For though we walk in the flesh, we do not war after the flesh, ₄for the weapons of our warfare are not carnal, but mighty through God to the pulling down of strong holds".*

Take note, "this is not a battle you are entering or will enter into, you are already in the battle regardless of whether you know it or not". You were already in the battle before you were born into this world; "the battle for your soul". God your Creator is asking for your soul to spend the rest of eternity with Him; to live with God forever in peace and glory. On the other hand, Satan the devil (your enemy) is fighting to rip your soul off the eternal destiny God have prepared for you, and to take your soul to the everlasting lake of fire which God has prepared for him and his demons. *Matthew 25:41 "Then shall He say also unto them on the left hand, depart from me, ye cursed into everlasting fire prepared for the devil and his angels".* **Now the decision is yours to make**. *2 Corinthians 6:2 "For He saith, I have heard thee in a time accepted, and in the day of salvation have I succoured thee: behold, now is the accepted time; behold, now is the day of salvation".* **Give your life to Jesus Christ today and received eternal life, or live to yourself and perish forever.** *Luke 13:3 "I tell you, nay; but except ye repent, ye shall all likewise perish".* *Luke 11:23 "He that is not with me is against me, and he that gathereth not with me scattereth".* This is my appeal to you today, please gather with Jesus Christ today (give your life to Jesus Christ today) so that you will not perish. *1 Corinthians 5:20 "Now then we are ambassadors for Christ, as though God did beseech you by us: we pray you in Christ's stead, be ye reconciled to God".* *Deuteronomy 30:19 "I call heaven and earth to record this day against you, that I have set before you, life and death, blessing and cursing: therefore choose life that both thou and thy seed may live".* This is your opportunity to make a decision for God, a decision you might not have another opportunity to make. Do not wait until it is too late. *Hebrews 9:27 "And as it is appointed unto men once to die, but after this the judgment".* *Joel 3:14 "Multitudes, multitudes, in the valley of decision: for the day of the Lord is near in the valley of decision".* **Get out of the multitude of undecided people today and make your own decision to follow and live for God through Jesus Christ; Jesus Christ will give you everlasting life.** *Romans 10:8-11 "But what saith it? The word is nigh thee, even in thy mouth, and in thy heart: that is, the word of faith, which we preach; ₉that if thou shalt confess with thy* mouth the Lord Jesus, and shalt believe in thine heart that God hath raised Him from the dead, thou shalt be saved. ₁₀For with the heart man believeth unto righteousness; and with the mouth confession is made unto salvation. ₁₁For the scripture saith, whosoever believeth on Him shall not be ashamed". John 1:12 "But as many as received Him, to them gave He power to become the sons of God, even to them that believe on His name". Would you become God's child today by giving your life to Jesus Christ? Revelation 3:20 "Look, I stand at the door and knock. If you hear my voice and open the door, I will come in, and we will share a meal together as friends". Jesus Christ is knocking at the door of your hearth; will you accept Him to today? "Be sincere". If you will accept Jesus Christ into your life today, please say the following prayer:

>*Lord Jesus, I accept that I am a sinner, and that I cannot save myself. Today, I ask you to forgive me of all my sins, and to cleanse me with your precious blood. Be my Lord and Savior. Lord Jesus, I invite you into my hearth, come and fill me with the Holy Spirit, and make me to live the rest of my days on this earth pleasing God. Thank you, Lord Jesus, for dying on Calvary cross to save me.   Amen.*

Chapter 5

Do I have a battle to fight?

The answer is a resounding yes. With God, sin of any kind will not enter into heaven. *Revelation 21:27 "And there shall in no wise enter into it anything that defileth, neither whatsoever worketh; abomination or maketh a lie, but they which are written in the book of life"*. If there is anything in this entire universe that God hates, then that thing is "***Sin***". God hates sin with the greatest passion ever. *Isaiah 61:8(NIV) "For I, the Lord, love justice; I hate robbery and iniquity. In my faithfulness I will reward them and make an everlasting covenant with them"*. *Numbers 14:18 "The Lord is longsuffering, and of great mercy, forgiving iniquity and transgression, and by no means clearing the guilty, visiting the iniquity of the fathers upon the children unto the third and fourth generation"*. This same God that is long-suffering and is great in mercy is the same God that visits the sins of the fathers upon the children unto the third and fourth generations. This shows the extent to which God hates sin. Do not joke about this, God meant everything He has said in His word. Regardless of what you are or what you are doing or have done to promote the purpose of God on this earth, God will never find peace with you if there is sin in you. Do not mistake God's grace and salvation for mankind to be God's weakness and tolerance to sin. No matter how God loves a man or anything, as long as that man or that thing is defiled with sin, God will cast away that man or that thing from His presence.

The heresy preached in some Churches of today says; "we are living in the time of grace, Jesus Christ has died for us; accept Jesus Christ, live your life and you will enter heaven when you die". No wonder many are disappointed beyond the grave. Your presence in the church pew does not guarantee your entrance into heaven, your name in the Church register does not guarantee your entrance into heaven, having favor with your pastor does not guarantee your entrance into heaven, your generosity and kindness does not guarantee your entrance into heaven. God is not joking. God will not change His standard for your sake. *Romans 2:11 "For there is no respect of persons with God"*. *Malachi 3:6ₐ "For I am the Lord, I change not"*. Make no mistake about this, the God that destroyed the whole earth by flood waters in the days of Noah, the God that rained down brimstone and fire on the inhabitants of Sodom and Gomorrah, the God that caused the ground to open up and bury Korah,

Dathan, and Abiram, together with their families and all their properties. He is still the God of today.

Many that are burning in hell fire today died thinking they were going to heaven simply because they were in a certain Church pew. A true Christian will always check with God to know the standing of his or her relationship with God. *2 Corinthians 13:5 "Examine yourselves, whether ye be in the faith; prove your own selves. Know ye not your own selves, how that Jesus Christ is in you, except ye be reprobates"*. Examine yourself now to see if there is sin in you and repent of your sins. Do not wait for God to tell you of your sins beyond the grave, because there might not be a second chance. This is the battle; *"**Fight for your soul, fight against Sin**"*. *Hebrews 12:4 "Ye have not yet resisted unto blood, striving against sin". Luke 13:24 "Strive to enter in at the strait gate: for many, I say unto you, will seek to enter in, and shall not be able". Luke 21:19 "In your patience possess ye your souls"*. You must strive (fight) to enter into the kingdom of heaven. You must fight against sin; because sin is what your enemy Satan, is using to stop you from entering into heaven. No one with sin in his or her life will enter heaven. Sin is the breaking of God's law or doing anything that displeases God. Sin irritates God.

You do not have to commit a crime against Satan in other for you to be his enemy. The devil hates God with a great passion, and therefore, the devil regards everyone created in the image of God to be his direct enemy. Because we were created in the image of God, the devil hates us with a great passion. The devil hates anything and everyone created by God. *2 Thessalonians 2:4ₐ "Who opposeth and exalteth himself above all that is called God, or that is worshipped"*. The devil hates us not only because we were created by God, but also because we were created in the image of God.

There is no way the devil can truly befriend any person, Satan is a deceiver. *John 10:10 "The thief cometh not, but for to steal, and to kill, and to destroy; I am come that they might have life and that they might have it more abundantly"*. The devil simply does not have the ability to love anyone. Satan is a thief, a killer, a deceiver and a destroyer of the human soul. The only thing the devil really does have to offer a man is the destruction of that man's soul. It is only God that truly loves you and me and has therefore sent His son Jesus Christ to die on the cross of cavalry for us. So that Jesus Christ can redeem us from sin and death through His blood that was shed on the cross for the sins of mankind. *Colossians 1:14 "In whom we have redemption through His blood, even the forgiveness of sins".*

Because the devil caused Adam and Eve to sin against God in the Garden of Eden, Adam and Eve acquired the nature of sin. So every man is naturally born into this world as a sinner. *Romans 3:23 "for all have sinned and come short of the glory of God".* Every man is naturally born in sin and therefore needs the blood of Jesus Christ for redemption and cleansing from sin. *Psalms 51:5 "Behold, I was shapen in iniquity; and in sin did my mother conceive me".* For only the blood of Jesus can wash away sin. Sin leads to death (eternal death; eternal separation from God). Ask God today to pour the blood of Jesus Christ upon you and to cleanse you from all sin and unrighteousness in your life. *1 John 1:8-9 "If we say that we have no sin, we deceive ourselves and the truth is not in us. 9 If we confess our sins, he is faithful and just to forgive us our sins, and to cleanse us from all unrighteousness".* Be sincere. *Matthew 18:14 "Even so it is not the will of your Father which is in heaven, that one of these little ones should perish".*

Chapter 6

How do I fight my battles?

This battle is spiritual and not physical. The battle against sin cannot be fought by your human strength, power or ability. The battle for your soul is entirely spiritual and therefore no man can conquer this battle without giving his or her life to Jesus Christ. For without Jesus Christ there is nothing a man can accomplish in the battle for his soul. *John 15:5 "I am the vine, ye are the branches: he that abideth in me, and I in him, the same bringeth forth much fruit: for without me ye can do nothing".*

Satan the devil is a spirit and the demons are spirits. It was the devil that first sinned in heaven. Lucifer was an angel of God; Lucifer rebelled against God when he decided to make himself equal with God. Because of his rebellion against God by wanting to make himself equal with God, Lucifer was cast out of heaven by God. *Isaiah 14:12-15 "How art thou fallen from heaven, O Lucifer, son of the morning! How art thou cut down to the ground, which didst weaken the nations! 13For thou hast said in thine heart, I will ascend into heaven, I will exalt my throne above the stars of God. I will sit also upon the mount of the congregation in the sides of the north. 14I will ascend above the heights of the clouds; I will be like the most high. 15Yet thou shalt be brought down to hell, to the sides of the pit". Revelation 12:7-9 "And there was war in heaven; Michael and his angels fought against the dragon; and the dragon fought and his angels, 8and prevailed not; neither was their place found any more in heaven. 9and the great dragon was cast out, that old serpent, called the devil, and Satan, which deceiveth the whole world; he was cast out into the earth, and his angels were cast out with him".*

Satan started his rebellion in heaven against God but he never succeeded. When Satan was cast out of heaven, he then started to fight against mankind in revenge for his excommunication from heaven by God. Satan was an angel in heaven created by God, but Satan chose to rebel against God's authority and supremacy. Satan wanted to make himself equal with God therefore God kicked him out of heaven, because no one can be equal to God.

The Bible made it clear to us that our battle against sin and the forces of darkness is spiritual. *Ephesians 6:12 "For we wrestle not against flesh and blood, but against principalities, against powers, against the rulers of the darkness of this world, against spiritual wickedness in high places"*. Though sometimes human beings can be possessed by evil spirits in other to accomplish satanic assignments on earth, yet those people are not to be seen as the enemy, they are mere vessels that the devil uses to carry out his assignments on earth. The devil is a spirit and therefore needs human vessels to carry out those assignments.

When I gave my life to the Lord Jesus Christ, within the first six months of being a born again Christian, I had series of attacks from the forces of darkness. I was not matured enough to handle spiritual matters. On a certain day after my quiet time at around 5am in the morning, I was about to go back to bed when I suddenly had an experience like somebody tapped me, saying, get up and pray they are attacking you. I sprang to my feet and I never knew how I busted into praying. I was intensely praying in the spirit, and after a moment I began to get an understanding of the personalities that had ganged against me. Two of my cousins born to my aunt, the older one a boy and the younger one a girl, both of them had been initiated into the witchcraft by their grandmother who had died years ago. Couple of months before this event, the younger one had publicly confessed of witchcraft, and her confession of witchcraft became news in the entire city. As I continued praying in tongues, the Lord made me to clearly see them in the spirit realm. They had actually plotted to kill me, and had therefore come that morning so they can kill me. They had reached this decision to kill me because, since I became a born again Christian, I had been constantly tormenting them with my prayers. In my encounter that faithful morning, I prayed about 30 to 45 minutes in tongues. Immediately after I finished my prayer, I took my cell phone and called my aunt. I asked my aunt to give her daughter the phone and that she was to put the phone on speaker. I asked her why they had come to attack me. She said it was her elder brother that had told her to join forces together with him and kill me because I was always tormenting them when I pray. I then cut off the call and called her elder brother. Upon picking my call, my statement was; "you shall not succeed, the Lord is my defender and protector". He responded sharply; are you calling me a witch? He immediately stopped the call and in the next minute he called my dad and mom telling them I had accused him of being a witch. His sharp respond confirmed to me that he knew exactly what he was doing and what had happened. Within the next 5 minutes the atmosphere became very uncomfortable for me, my dad and mom had come to my room to tell me that my cousin had just called them complaining that I called him a witch. After that entire scenario, I realized that I had acted immaturely. The Lord had revealed to me their evil plans that morning, the Spirit of God had inspired me to pray fervently, I had received confirmation in my spirit that they were been defeated. All I needed to do then was praise and thank God for the victory He had given me. But out of spiritual immaturity, I created unnecessary problems for myself. My dad warned me that if I continue embarrassing him in that manner, he will stop me from praying in his house. Those individuals that are being possessed by satanic powers to do the works of Satan on this earth are merely being used as instruments by the devil; they are not to be seen as the devil himself.

Jesus rebuked the spirit that was inspiring Peter to plead with Jesus not to go to the cross. *Matthew 16:23 "But he turned, and said unto Peter, get thee behind me, Satan: thou art an offence unto me: for thou savourest not the things that be of God, but those that be of men".* Jesus was not referring directly to Peter as being Satan, Jesus was rebuking the spirit that was speaking through Peter. The devil wanted to use that statement to make Jesus to be afraid of the pain He was to endure on the across, because Jesus knew exactly the gruesome pain that He had to go through. Remember when Jesus asked his disciples about who they think He was; peter's answer at that time was inspired by the Holy Spirit. *Matthew 16:16-18 "And Simon Peter answered and said; thou art the Christ, the Son of the living God. 17And Jesus answered and said unto him, blessed art thou, Simon Barjona, for flesh and blood hath not revealed it unto thee, but my Father which is in heaven. 18And I say also unto thee, that thou art Peter, and upon this rock; I will build my church and the gates of hell shall not prevail against it".* Here Jesus Christ commended, blessed, prophesied, and ordained Peter after his response, because peter's response here was inspired by the Holy Spirit. Right after Peter's responds; declaring Jesus Christ as the Messiah and the son of God, when the other disciples were still confused about the true identity of Jesus Christ. The Lord Jesus Christ handed over to Peter the assignment of preaching on the day of Pentecost. We can clearly see the difference that Peter's response in Matthew 16:23 was not inspired by the Holy Spirit but by the devil.

A brother once told me in a Bible study class that one of his youngest daughter who was under the age of ten had confessed that she was a witch and that she was responsible for all the problems they had been experiencing in the home. While under the power of God, the evil spirit inside the little girl manifested and claimed to have been in existence centuries ago. Someone will now ask the question, how can a small girl under the age of ten know this much? The fact is; it was the spirit that claimed to have been in existence centuries ago which possessed the little girl, and was using her to wreck-havoc on her family. One will clearly see that the little girl was not in control of herself. She was only been used by the spirit that possessed her, and it was the spirit which had possessed her that was pushing her into doing whatever she did.

The Bible lets us understand that God is a spirit and that God's power is supreme above all other powers. *John 4:24 "God is a Spirit and they that worship Him must worship Him in spirit and in truth". Psalms 62:11 "God hath spoken once, twice have I heard this, that power belongeth unto God".* Also the Bible made us know that God is love, and that there is nothing impossible with God. *1 John 4:8 "He that loveth not knoweth not God; for God is love". Luke1:37 "For with God nothing shall be impossible".* Therefore, if a person is wise enough, he or she will surrender his/her life to Jesus Christ who has won the victory over sin, death and Satan, because the power of Jesus Christ is supreme over Satan and all his demons.

Ephesians 1:19-22 "And what is the exceeding greatness of His power to us-ward who believe, according to the working of His mighty power 20which He wrought in Christ, when He raised Him from the dead, and set Him at His own right hand in the heavenly places. 21Far above all principality, and power, and might, and dominion, and every name that is named, not only in this world, but also in that which is to come; 22and hath put all things under His feet, and gave Him to be the head over all things to the church". Philippians 2:9-10 "Wherefore God also hath highly exalted Him, and given Him a name which is above every name. 10That at the name of Jesus every knee should bow, of things in heaven, and things in earth, and things under the earth; 11and that every tongue should confess that Jesus Christ is Lord, to the glory of God the Father".

Common sense should let humanity realize that we need God, if we are to have true peace, love, and true success in anything upon this earth. God created the universe, God created mankind, God's power is supreme, God knows all things and God can do anything at anytime and anywhere, and there is no power that can be compared with the power of God. God is good, God is kind, God is loving, God is caring, God is merciful, God created man in His own very image; everything we see today was created by God and for God; the heavens, the earth, the sun, the moon, the stars, the air we breathe, the water we drink, the food we eat. All these things should let humanity realize that God loves us beyond our understanding.

If there is anyone in this universe that humanity owns an obligation to, it should be God; because God created us in His own very image, and has put His breath in us, and that is the reason why we are alive today. *Genesis 2:7 "And the Lord God formed man of the dust of the ground, and breathed into his nostrils the breath of life; and man became a living soul"*. The breath in you is absolutely God's own property and God will take it back one day without even consulting you. *Ecclesiastes 12:7 "Then shall the dust return to the earth as it was, and the spirit shall return unto God who gave it". Psalm 103:15 "As for man, his days are as grass: as a flower of the field, so he flourisheth". 1 peter 1:24 "For all flesh is as grass, and all the glory of man as the flower of grass. The grass withereth, and the flower thereof falleth away"*. No matter the extent to which a man rises in power, fame, knowledge, wealth, and achievements in this life, he or she will one day die just like any pauper will die. This shows how much each person needs to be in a good relationship with God.

No man can serve two masters; you must choose one. *Matthew 6:24 "No man can serve two masters: for either he will hate the one, and love the other; or else he will hold to the one, and despise the other. Ye cannot serve God and mammon". Joshua 24:15 "And if it seem evil unto you to serve the Lord, choose you this day whom ye will serve; whether the gods which your fathers served that were on the other side of the flood, or the gods of the Amorites, in whose land ye dwell: but as for me and my house, we will serve the Lord"*. Like Joshua, everyone has to make his or her own choice to either serve the true God or not. *John 8:34 "He that committeth sin is of the devil; for the devil sinneth from the beginning. For this purpose the Son of God was manifested, that He might destroy the works of the devil"*.

Chapter 7

You must be born-again.

Heaven is God's own kingdom and therefore entrance into heaven is based mainly on God's own standards and approval. The Jesus Christ, during His earthly ministry gave us insight into what exactly qualifies a man for entrance into heaven. Jesus Christ said that; except a man be born again, he shall not see the kingdom of God. *John 3:3 "Jesus answered and said unto him, verily, verily, I say unto thee, except a man be born again, he cannot see the kingdom of God".*

Born-again is a regeneration process of the human spirit and soul that can only be done by the Holy Spirit of God; a spiritual transformation which the Holy Spirit alone can do in a person's life. *Colossians 1:13 "Who hath delivered us from the power of darkness, and hath translated us into the kingdom of His dear Son".* This makes it clear that anyone that does not have the Holy Spirit of God in him/her does not belong to God. *Romance 8:9 "But ye are not in the flesh, but in the Spirit, if so be that the Spirit of God dwell in you, now if any man have not the Spirit of Christ, he is none of His".* Stop deceiving yourself. The Bible says John the Baptist baptized with water, but Jesus Christ baptizes with the Holy Spirit and fire. *Matthew 3:11"I indeed baptize you with water unto repentance: but He that cometh after me is mightier than I, whose shoes I am not worthy to bear: He shall baptize you with the Holy Ghost, and with fire". John 14:16 "And I will pray the Father, and He shall give you another Comforter, that He may abide with you forever; 17even the Spirit of truth; whom the world cannot receive, because it seeth Him not, neither knoweth Him. But ye know him; for He dwelleth with you, and shall be in you".* This is no joke, if you do not have the Holy Spirit living in you and you call yourself a Child of God, you are deceiving yourself. The Lord Jesus Christ, in John 3:3 did not say "unless you are a Christian you cannot enter the kingdom of heaven" the Lord Jesus Christ said "unless you are born again, you will not see the kingdom of God". If you are going to church, dedicated and committed, and you do not have the Holy Spirit of God in you, please go on your knees now and pray fervently asking Jesus Christ to baptize you with the Holy Spirit. Every born again is a Christian, but not every Christian is a born again. To be born again is the first requirement for entering the kingdom of heaven. If you do not have the Holy Spirit living in you, then you do not know Jesus Christ, and you do not have a relationship with Him. *2 Corinthians 3:17 "Now the Lord is that Spirit: and where the Spirit of the Lord is, there is liberty".* That means if anyone does not have the Holy Spirit of God in him or her, that person is not saved. As a guarantee of God's salvation upon any man or woman, God puts His Holy Spirit upon that man or that woman. *2 Corinthians 5:5(NLT) "God Himself has prepared us for this, and as a guarantee He has given us His Holy Spirit".*

Heaven is where God's throne is, and from heaven God rules the earth. The Bible clearly reveals to us that God dwells in heaven, meaning, heaven is God's home. Be careful, God is not your grand pa that you can bump into heaven as you want. Consider heaven to be God's house, and God will only allow those He is pleased with into His own house. Remember, God have angels (the most powerful security agents in the entire universe). Do not just be excited about the miracles you see or the gifts that God have placed in you; a truly born again Christian will always check with God to see if he or she is still walking in God's will. If there is anyone to be deceived in the entire universe, it's certainly not God. *Galatians 6:7-8 ",Be not deceived; God is not mocked: for whatsoever a man soweth, that shall he also reap. ₈For he that soweth to his flesh shall of the flesh reap corruption; but he that soweth to the Spirit shall of the Spirit reap life everlasting".*

Being a church goer is entirely different from being born again. Church goers do not allow the word of God to transform the way they live. Instead, they want to change God's word to fit their own life style. Being in a church congregation does not mean you are saved. A clear guarantee to let you know that you are born again; is the presence of the Holy Spirit in you, to which you do not need any human confirmation. *Romance 8:16 "The Spirit Himself beareth witness with our spirit, that we are the children of God".* The very moment the Holy Spirit starts to living in you, you will not need a confirmation from people because the Holy Spirit Himself will bear witness with your spirit, and you will see the changes that will take place in your life. Stop being a Church goer and be born again.

Chapter 8

You must have Faith in God.

Faith, the bed rock upon which man's relationship with God is laid. From creation until now God has been looking for men and women that would believe in Him, His word, His power, and His promises. Faith is beyond recognizing or knowing that God is the creator of this universe. Faith is beyond knowing or acknowledging that God exists. Faith goes beyond mere recognition of God's greatness, existence, and ownership of the universe. God is longing to strike a deal with men and women who despite the circumstances they see or face; still do believe in God's word and promises to them. Faith is not what you think, faith is not what you see, faith is not what the situation is or seems to be like, faith is not what you or others view the situation to be. Faith is that absolute believe and trust, total dependence on what God has said, and what God has promised to do. In *Hebrews 11:1(NLT), we are told what faith actually means. "Faith is the confidence that what we hope for will actually happen; it gives us assurance about things we cannot see".* Head knowledge is different from faith, imagination is different from faith, views and opinions are different from faith, experiments and theories are different from faith. Faith in itself is naturally activated and cannot be manipulated. Faith stirs and establishes once confidence in what really is not visible to the natural sight.

The Bible says no man has ever seen God with his natural eyes. *1 John 4:12 "no man hath seen God at any time: if we love one another, God dwelleth in us and His love is perfected in us".* God is a spirit and therefore the natural eyes of a man cannot see God. In other for a man or woman to walk with God, that man or woman must walk in faith which only God can grant a person. Faith is that ability to depend on the spoken word of God regardless of the counteracting situation that may exist. In a man's walk with God, faith is more than essential. *Hebrews 11:6 "But without faith it is impossible to please Him: for he that cometh to God must believe that He is, and that He is a rewarder of them that diligently seek Him".* The Scripture tells us in *Romans 14: 23 that, "whatsoever one does that is not of faith is sin".* If it is impossible to please God without faith, then one must consider faith to be very vital before God. For it is only through faith, that we are saved. *Ephesians 2:8 "For by grace are ye saved through faith; and that not of yourselves: it is the gift of God".*

Millions have hard the gospel of Jesus Christ preached to them in a simple and clear manner that they understood, but not all of them believed unto salvation. It is God gives that special grace that stirs up faith in a person to believe in the death and resurrection of Jesus Christ as the messiah and son of God. For no man can receive God's salvation without faith.

Men and women of faith in Bible days were able to accomplish greater things because of their faith in God. For a person to have strong faith in God, that person needs to know God. Your faith stops at the level to which you personally know God. The extent to which you know God is the extent to which your faith can go. *Daniel 11:32ᵦ "but the people that do know their God shall be strong, and do exploits".* Men and women that were able to do exploit for the kingdom of God were people that had great faith in God. Knowing God is not merely acknowledging His existence, His power, His dominion, or the mighty works God is doing or has done. Knowing God is to know the difference between; what "the will" of God is and what is not "the will" of God, and doing "the will of God". The prayer of the Apostle Peter for every Christian; is to grow in grace, and in the knowledge of our Lord Jesus Christ. *2 Peter 3:18 "But grow in; grace and in the knowledge of our Lord and savior Jesus Christ. To Him be glory both now and forever, Amen".* This shows that for a Christian to be strong enough to do exploit, that Christina must grow in grace and in the knowledge of our Lord Jesus Christ. The Christian that refuses to grow in grace and in the knowledge of God will never be able to do exploit, because he or she will not have the faith that is required to be strong enough for doing exploit things.

Your faith in God should develop in you the guts you need to face the devil and his cohorts; and prevail over them. God is still looking for men and women that are bold enough to take the battle to the gates of the enemy. *Isaiah 6:8 "Also I heard the voice of the Lord, saying, whom shall I send, and who will go for us? Then said I, here am I; send me".* Until the day the prophet Isaiah saw God, he was a timid and lukewarm prophet. But when the prophet Isaiah finally saw the glory of the Almighty God, he developed the faith his ministry was lacking. God is still asking the question today "whom shall I send, and who will go for us"? God is still looking for men and women into whose hands He can entrust great assignments to be accomplished for His kingdom. God is looking for men and women that He can boast of in the presence of His enemies. *Job 1:8 (NIV) "then the LORD said to Satan: have you considered my servant Job? There is no one on earth like him; he is blameless and upright, a man who fears God and shuns evil."* God was boasting of His servant Job to the devil, that there was no man righteous like Job in all the earth, a man with integrity and one who fears God and hates evil. Did you take notice of that? God didn't discuss it first with Job before boasting to Satan about Job. You want to know why? God trusted Job, and God knew Job will not disappoint Him. How many of us are there today in the body of Christ that God can rely on to do His will, and to boast of them in front of His enemies? God is still searching for men and women with such caliber of faith today; who will stand against the enemy and set the prisoners free, deliver the captives, heal the wounded, bind the broken hearted and preach the gospel of peace to the poor. God is ready to unleash His power. All the Lord is looking for is; men and women who are ready to build alliance with God and show forth His glory in this earth.

Chapter 9

You must be filled with the Holy Spirit.

Heaven is not a place meant for radicals, heaven is a place prepared for prepared people. The Bible tells us about the unique oneness of the trinity; God the father, God the son, and God the Holy Spirit, is one. *Ephesians 4:5 "One Lord, one faith, one baptism, ₆and one God and Father of all; who is above all, and through all, and in you all".* In the Trinity, God the Father said the word in creation (God the son "Jesus Christ" is that word), and God the Holy Spirit accomplished (bring the word of God the Father to pass). *Genesis 1:2 "And God said, let there be light, and there was light".* When "God said" let there be light, His word went fort, and God the Holy Spirit brings it to pass. *John 1:1 "In the beginning was the Word, and the Word was with God, and the Word was God; ₂the same was in the beginning with God".* *Revelation 19:13 "And He was clothed with a vesture dipped in blood: and His name is called; the Word of God".* *Isaiah 55:11 "So shall my word be that goeth forth out of my mouth; it shall not return unto me void, but it shall accomplish that which I please, and it shall prosper in the thing whereto I sent it".* Jesus Christ is the word of God.

After the fall of man in the Garden of Eden, man became an enemy of God. God in His infinite mercy decided to send His son Jesus Christ in to this sinful world as a sacrifice; to die for the sins of mankind. So that mankind can be reconciled with his creator again. *Romans 5:10 "For if when we were enemies we were reconciled to God by the death of His Son, much more, being reconciled, we shall be saved by His life".* The Holy Spirit of God was the one that brought about the birth of Jesus Christ. *Luke 1:35(NLT) "The angel replied, the Holy Spirit will come upon you, and the power of the most high will overshadow you, so the baby to be born will be holy, and He will be called the son of God".* During the earthly ministry of our Lord Jesus Christ, God the Father gave Him the Holy Spirit to help Him accomplish His earthly ministry. *John 1:32 "Then John testified, "I saw the Holy Spirit descending like a dove from heaven and resting upon Him".* *John 3:34 "For He whom God hath sent speaketh the words of God: for God giveth not the Spirit by measure unto Him".* Jesus Christ was filled with the fullness of God's Spirit. Therefore, the ministry of Jesus Christ on earth was unique. *Matthew 7:28-29 "And it came to pass, when Jesus had ended these sayings, the people were astonished at His doctrine: ₂₉for He taught them as one having authority, and not as the scribes".*

Remember when the Lord Jesus Christ was just a boy, He knew the word of God, because He is the word of God, but during that time, His time for ministry had not yet come because He hadn't receive the Holy Spirit yet. *Luke 2:46-47 "And it came to pass, that after three days they found Him in the temple, sitting in the midst of the doctors, both hearing them, and asking them questions. 47 And all that heard Him were astonished at His understanding and answers".* Our Lord Jesus Christ did not do any miracle until after His baptism, when He received the fullness of the Holy Spirit. Immediately, His ministry started. This shows how important it is for every Christian to be filled with the Holy Spirit.

In His final teachings, our Lord Jesus Christ told His disciples that it was necessary for Him to go so that He could send the Holy Spirit for the church. *John 16:7 "Nevertheless I tell you the truth; it is expedient for you that I go away: for if I go not away, the Comforter will not come unto you; but if I depart, I will send Him unto you".* The Lord Jesus Christ said that when the Holy Spirit comes; He will teach, guide and bring to the remembrance of every believer the truth and the will of God. *John 16:13 "Howbeit when He, the Spirit of truth, is come, He will guide you into all truth: for He shall not speak of Himself; but whatsoever He shall hear, that shall He speak: and He will show you things to come".* This shows how essential it is for a Christian to be filled with the Holy Spirit of God. "As faith without work is dead, so also, a Christian without the Holy Spirit is dead". If a man or a woman is in a church pew and does not have the Holy Spirit of God present in his or her life, he or she is not a Christian. The Holy Spirit is the administrator, CEO, and General Manager of the church (a Christian's life). *1 Corinthians 3:16-17 "Know ye not that ye are the temple of God, and that the Spirit of God dwelleth in you? 17 If any man defile the temple of God, him shall God destroy; for the temple of God is holy, which temple ye are".*

The life of every born again Christian must be filled, guided, and lead by the Holy Spirit. *Galatians 2:20 "I am crucified with Christ: nevertheless I live; yet not I, but Christ liveth in me: and the life which I now live in the flesh I live by the faith of the Son of God, who loved me, and gave Himself for me".* Jesus Christ came into the earth and died for the sins of mankind in other that, anyone that will believe in Him will have access to eternal life through His blood. After His death on the cross and His resurrection on the third day from death, Jesus Christ went back to heaven to meet His father. *Mark 16:19 "So then after the Lord had spoken unto them, He was received up into heaven, and sat on the right hand of God".* The devil is only afraid of Christians that are filled with the Holy Spirit. Any one claiming to be a Christian and does not have the Holy Spirit living in him or her, is not a Christian and does not belong to God, neither does he or she knows God. *Romans 8:9 "But ye are not in the flesh, but in the Spirit, if so be that the Spirit of God dwell in you, now if any man have not the Spirit of Christ, he is none of His".*

As a proof of God's acceptance and salvation upon any individual, God seals the person with His Holy Spirit. If you are going to church and you do not have the Holy Spirit of God living in you, that shows you are not born again and you do not belong to God's kingdom. *John 3:3 "Jesus answered and said unto him, Verily, verily, I say unto thee, except a man be born again, he cannot see the kingdom of God".* The government of every country provides each of its citizens a means of identification to prove their right of citizenship. Likewise God gives His Holy Spirit to each of His children to prove a right of son-ship or daughter-ship, and a right of citizenship in heaven. *John 1:12 "But as many as received Him, to them gave He power to become the sons of God, even to them that believe on His name". 1 John 3:1-3 "Behold, what manner of love the Father hath bestowed upon us, that we should be called the sons of God: therefore the world knoweth us not, because it knew Him not. ₂Beloved, now are we the sons of God: and it doth not yet appear what we shall be, but we know that, when He shall appear, we shall be like Him; for we shall see Him as He is. ₃And every man that hath this hope in him purifieth himself, even as He is pure". Romans 8:14-17 "For as many as are led by the Spirit of God, they are the sons of God. ₁₅For ye have not received the spirit of bondage again to fear; but ye have received the Spirit of adoption, whereby we cry, Abba, Father. ₁₆The Spirit Himself beareth witness with our spirit, that we are the children of God: ₁₇and if children, then heirs; heirs of God, and joint-heirs with Christ; if so be that we suffer with Him, that we may be also glorified together". Philippians 3:20 "But our citizenship is in heaven, and we eagerly await a savior from there: the Lord Jesus Christ".* This is not a joke, if you are claiming to be a Christian and you do not have the Holy Spirit living in you, please go on your knees now and ask the Lord Jesus Christ to baptize you with the Holy Spirit now. *Matthew 3:11 "I indeed baptize you with water unto repentance: but He that cometh after me is mightier than I, whose shoes I am not worthy to bear: He shall baptize you with the Holy Ghost and with fire".* Desire the Holy Spirit today and the Lord Jesus Christ will fill you. Be sincere.

After His resurrection from the grave, one of the last statements our Lord Jesus Christ made to His disciples; was for them to wait in the upper room until they receive the Holy Spirit. *Acts 1:8 "But ye shall receive power, after that the Holy Ghost is come upon you: and ye shall be witnesses unto me both in Jerusalem, and in all Judaea, and in Samaria, and unto the uttermost part of the earth".* From the events of *Acts 2:1-4 "And when the day of Pentecost was fully come, they were all* with one accord in one place. *₂And suddenly there came a sound from heaven as of a rushing mighty wind, and it filled the house where they were sitting. ₃And there appeared unto them cloven tongues like as of fire, and it sat upon each of them. ₄And they were all filled with the Holy Ghost, and began to speak with other tongues, as the Spirit gave them utterance"*. You noticed that a tremendous change took place in the life of each of the 120 individuals that received the baptism of the Holy Spirit on that day of Pentecost. Each of the disciples became bold and strong enough to face the crowd and preach the gospel of Jesus Christ. The same peter that denied Jesus Christ, his 3 year-long master, friend and savior before a common servant girl, was now able to preach a single message and 3,000 souls were saved. *John 18:17 "Then saith the damsel that kept the door unto Peter, art not thou also one of this man's disciples? He saith, I am not "*. *Acts 2:41 "Then they that gladly received his word were baptized: and the same day there were added unto them about three thousand souls"*. That same peter was now bold enough to talk right into the face of the elders that nothing can stop him from preaching the gospel of Jesus Christ. *Acts 5:27-29 "And when they had brought them, they set them before the council: and the high priest asked them, ₂₈saying, did not we straitly command you that ye should not teach in this name? And behold, ye have filled Jerusalem with your doctrine, and intend to bring this man's blood upon us. ₂₉Then Peter and the other apostles answered and said, we ought to obey God rather than men"*. After his encounter with the Holy Spirit, Peter was now the man that rejoiced after been whipped severely by the temple leaders for preaching in the name of Jesus Christ. *Acts 5:40-42 "And to him they agreed: and when they had called the apostles, and beaten them, they commanded that they should not speak in the name of Jesus, and let them go. ₄₁And they departed from the presence of the council, rejoicing that they were counted worthy to suffer shame for His name. ₄₂And daily in the temple, and in every house, they ceased not to teach and preach Jesus Christ"*. The same peter that was most times sleeping when the Lord Jesus Christ was praying, after Peter received the Holy Spirit, Peter became a man of prayer. *Mathew 26:40 "And he cometh unto the disciples, and findeth them asleep, and saith unto Peter, what, could ye not watch with me one hour?"* But when the Holy Spirit came upon the apostles, prayer, fasting, and preaching the Lord Jesus Christ became their focus. *Acts 6:2 "But we will give ourselves continually to prayer, and to the ministry of the word"*.

You cannot serve God with your human strength or knowledge. Every true Christian is filled with the spirit of God; only those filled with the Holy Spirit of God, are true Christians. For any Christian to fulfill the purpose of God upon his or her life, he or she must be filled with the Holy Spirit. Every Christian needs the Holy Spirit to live above sin; living above sin is not being controlled by the sinful nature anymore.

In other for any Christian to know the will of God, he or she must be filled with the Holy Spirit. You cannot live a life pleasing to God without having the Holy Spirit of God dwelling in you. The Holy Spirit leads the Christian into doing the will of God, the Holy Spirit also helps the Christian to identify and run away from what is not God's will. *John 16:8 "And when He is come, He will reprove the world of sin, and of righteousness, and of judgment".* For you to please God, you need the spirit of God. *Philippians 2:13 "For it is God which worketh in you: both to will and to do of His good pleasure".* God made man for His pleasure; therefore, man ought to please God. God regards anything that does not please Him to be abhorrent unto Him. *Colossians1:16 "For by Him were all things created, that are in heaven, and that are in earth, visible and invisible, whether they be thrones, or dominions, or principalities, or powers: all things were created by Him, and for Him".*

Chapter 10

You must know the word of God.

It is very important to Study the word of God's as a Christian and a follower of Jesus Christ. The Holy Bible is God's spoken word to mankind. The Bible was inspired by the Holy Spirit of God; the Holy Spirit of God inspired chosen men to write the Bible. *2 Timothy 3:16-17 "All scripture is given by inspiration of God, and is profitable for doctrine, for reproof, for correction, for instruction in righteousness: 17that the man of God may be perfect; thoroughly furnished unto all good works".* The Bible is complete, pure, and without any error. *Psalm 119:140 "Thy word is very pure: therefore thy servant loveth it". Verse 142 "Thy righteousness is an everlasting righteousness, and thy law is the truth". Verse 144 "The righteousness of thy testimonies is everlasting: give me understanding, and I shall live". Verse 160 "Thy word is true from the beginning: and every one of thy righteous judgments endures forever".*

Many Christians say the Bible contradicts itself; that is a lie, a deception from the pit of hell; do not be deceived by the devil. God meant every word He said in the scriptures, and it is not the place of man to argue God's word. *Mark 13:31 "Heaven and earth shall pass away; but my words shall not pass away".* Truly born again Christians do not argue the word of God; they obey the word of God. Arguing and questioning the Holy Scriptures is a clear indication that a person lacks the fear of God. From Genesis 1:1, down to Revelations 22:21, the duty of mankind is to obey. *Ecclesiastes 12:13 "Let us hear the conclusion of the whole matter: Fear God, and keep His commandments: for this is the whole duty of man".* God, in most cases speaks in parables. Therefore, it takes the spirit of God to give a clear interpretation of God's word. *Mark 4:34-35 "And with many such parables spake He the word unto them, as they were able to hear it. 34But without a parable spake He not unto them: and when they were alone, He expounded all things to His disciples".* This verse shows exactly how important it is for a Christian to daily have a personal Bible study. If you do not understand any verse in the Holy Scriptures, ask the Holy Spirit to teach you, that is one of the reasons why God sent His Holy Spirit to into His Church. *2 Corinthians 2:10-11 "But God hath revealed them unto us by His Spirit: for the Spirit searcheth all things, yea the deep things of God. 11For what man knoweth the things of a man, save the spirit of man which is in him? Even so the things of God knoweth no man, but the Spirit of God".*

Many people interpret certain parts of the scripture in different ways. Therefore, it is good that a Christian depends on the Holy Spirit for a clear interpretation of the Scriptures. God' word is meant to transform a person's lifestyle in other to match the nature of God; it is not the person that should transform the word of God to match his or her own lifestyle. One of the secrets behind King David's success in walking with God, and in finding favor with God was that; King David entirely trusted and depended on the word of God. God is not looking for men and women that will argue what He says, God is looking for men and women that will trust and obey all what God has said, all that God is saying, and all what God will say. God is not looking for editors of His word; God is looking for men and women that will trust and obey His word. God is not looking for people to interpret His word as they think, or to please other people or themselves; God is looking for men and women that will interpret His word as He meant it to be. God's decision is firm about every portion of His word, and this is one of God's ways of knowing those who truly believe and love Him, from the hypocrites. *2 Timothy 2:19 "Nevertheless the foundation of God standeth sure; having this seal the Lord knoweth them that are His. And, let everyone that nameth the name of Christ depart from iniquity". John 14:15 "If ye love me, keep my commandments".*

A truly born again Christian (not the one that claims to be born again when he or she is really not) is sealed with the Holy Spirit of God, and departs from evil. Remember, no one can deceive God, if you love God, you will trust and obey God's word. Stop the shouting and jumping, and start submitting yourself to God by obeying His word. God is not moved by your shouting, jumping and pretense; God is moved by your obedience. *Mathew 7:21 "Not every one that saith unto me, Lord, Lord, shall enter into the kingdom of heaven; but he that doeth the will of my Father which is in heaven".* Stop arguing God's word; only critics and opponents argue, children and servants do not argue; children and servants obey. *Isaiah 45:9-10 "Woe unto him that striveth with his maker! Let the potsherd strive with the potsherds of the earth. Shall the clay say to him that fashioneth it, what makest thou? Or thy work, he hath no hands?"* Stop arguing with God's word and start obeying it. God is looking for followers, not instructors. *1 Corinthians 2:19 "For who hath known the mind of the Lord, that he may instruct Him? But we have the mind of Christ".* Christians are meant to have the mind of Jesus Christ, and not to instruct God.

Some Christians categorize the Bible into; which part to obey, and which part not to obey. Both the New Testament and the Old Testament of the Holy Scriptures is God's word; therefore, mankind's duty is to obey both the Old and New Testaments of the Bible.

A Christian is to study and meditate on the word of God daily. It is God's will that His children study and understand His word. This cannot be possible without the Holy Spirit. If a man is to know the will of God and to please God, that man needs to study and understand God's word. By studying God's word, we learn about God's purpose, likes and dislikes, God's plan for humanity and the rest of His creation, God's promises and His love for us, God's plan of salvation and judgment, God's goodness and power, God's delight, and the things that displeases God. Also, as we study the word of God, we learn of the devices of the devil. King David knew this secret: therefore, he gave himself the more time to study the word of God. King David always said; 'he delighted himself in the word of God'. As we study the word of God, it shows our love and desire for God. Studying God's word indicates a person's thirst, longing, and love for God's righteousness, holiness, and purity. *Psalm 42:1-2 "As the hart panteth after the water brooks, so panteth my soul after thee, O God. ₂My soul thirsts for God, for the living God: when shall I come and appear before God?" Psalm 119:15-16 "I will meditate in thy precepts, and have respect unto thy ways. ₁₆I will delight myself in thy statutes: I will not forget thy word"*. It is very clear that when we study the word of God, we get to know God's will for us, God's purpose for us, God's power in us, God's promises to us, God's love for us, and God's plans for us.

We also need to study the word of God to prove whether these things are so. *Acts 17:11 "These were more noble than those in Thessalonica, in that they received the word with all readiness of mind, and searched the scriptures daily, whether those things were so"*.

Christianity is a covenant relationship between a person and God through the sacrificial death and resurrection of Jesus Christ. How can you get into a covenant or agreement with someone without you even knowing the details of the agreement you are into? When we study the word of God, we know the details of the covenant relationship we have with God through the blood of His son Jesus Christ, we also know the details of what God is expecting of us.

As we study the word of God, we remind ourselves daily about the covenant we have with God. *John 5:39 "Search the scriptures; for in them ye think ye have eternal life: and they are they which testify of me"*. The Scriptures testify of Jesus Christ in whom we have eternal life. The Bible is God's memorandum of agreement with His children. With all of your busy schedules, spend at least 30 minutes each day to study and meditate upon God's word; a way of reassuring yourself daily of the covenant relationship you have with God. Do not be a blind Christian; one that does not know the details of his covenant relationship with God. If you don't study the word of God, you will not know the premises, plans, propose, love, and provisions of God for you.

Chapter 11

You must know your authority in Christ Jesus.

As we have learned in the previous chapter that a Christian should study the word of God. It is only when we study the word of God, then we are able to discover the authority we have in the name of Jesus Christ. If a Christian doesn't know his or her authority in Jesus Christ, that Christian is like a soldier in the front with no weapon. How can a person go into battle against his or her enemy when he or she does not know what weapons are available to him or her. *Luke 14:31 "Or what king, going to make war against another king, sitteth not down first, and consulteth whether he be able with ten thousand to meet him that cometh against him with twenty thousand?"* Do not turn yourself into a casualty in the hands of Satan and his demons. We are already born in to the battle, you cannot escape this battle, this is a no retreat no surrender spiritual warfare we are in. If you retreat, you will be a casualty to Satan and his demons, if you surrender, you will be a casualty to Satan and his demons.

Humanity is caught in the middle of the longest and fiercest war ever between two spiritual forces with both sides aiming at getting your soul. God, your creator is fighting to defend you from losing your soul to Satan and his demons. Satan and his demons are trying to drag your soul into the eternal fire God has prepared for them as a judgment for their rebellion against God. God has made every weapon available to the believer in other to overcome the kingdom of darkness. Every power of God is made available to the believer. If you are a true child of God, then be rest assured, you have all of God's power available to you; the entire kingdom of heaven is in support of every Christian.

Make no mistake about this, no man or woman can escape this battle. *Luke 13:24 "Strive to enter in at the strait gate; for many, I say unto you, will seek to enter in, and shall not be able"*. In this verse the Lord Jesus Christ said, "many will seek (try) to enter into the kingdom of heaven but shall not be able. What many Christians believe today is; because Jesus Christ has die for them and they have believed in Jesus Christ as their Lord and Savior; that is the end, they are saved. But the truth is, in God's salvation plan for mankind, there are also responsibilities God has given to mankind. If there were no responsibilities for mankind in God's salvation plan, then God would have taken every believer strait to heaven the very moment they get saved. But then after you believed and confessed Jesus Christ as your Lord and Savior you are still on earth, this shows you have an assignment to fulfill. God's agenda is to build an army of saints that can root out, pull down, destroy, and throw down wickedness, and to build and plant righteousness. *Jeremiah1:10 "See, I have this day set thee over the nations and over the kingdoms, to root out, and to pull down, and to destroy, and to throw down, to build, and to plant". Luke 10:19 "Behold, I give unto you power to tread on serpents and scorpions, and over all the power of the enemy: and nothing shall by any means hurt you"*. Our Lord Jesus Christ repeatedly reminded us of the power and authority He has given to His church. Every power of God is available to the Christian for use, but most Christians are not aware of God's power been made available to them.

If you don't know your authority in Jesus Christ, you are like a financially rich person dying of hunger because he or she is not aware of having enough money to buy some food, or you are like a child begging his mother to please have him as her child when in fact he/she is already her child. Ignorance of the law is no excuse. Likewise, being ignorant of your rights will not prevent you from going through the sufferings. If you look down on knowledge, you will suffer for your foolishness. *Hosea 4:6 "My people are destroyed for lack of knowledge: because thou hast rejected knowledge, I will also reject thee, that thou shalt be no priest to me: seeing thou hast forgotten the law of thy God, I will also forget thy children"*. Lack of knowledge in this life can cost you eternity, your life, your joy, your peace and everything.

Most Christians are afraid of the devil attacking them because they do not know their authority in Jesus Christ. If you are a Christian filled with the Holy Spirit, then the devil is the one to fear you. *2 Timothy 1:7 "For God hath not given us the spirit of fear: but of power and of love, and of a sound mind"*. *Proverbs 28:1 "The wicked flee when no man pursueth: but the righteous are bold as a lion"*. Wickedness is always associated with horror and fear. A Christian is meant to be bold and powerful. The devil is a deceiver and will always try to intimidate you in order to subdue you, but those that do know their authority in Christ Jesus will always prevail and will never be intimidated by the devil. *Daniel 11:32 "And such as do wickedly against the covenant shall he corrupt by flatteries: but the people that do know their God shall be strong, and do exploits"*. Only those Christians that do know their God will know the power of their God. David knew God and the power of God, and that was why David was able to defeat the giant-Goliath. *1 Samuel 17:45 "Then said David to the Philistine, thou comest to me with a sword, and with a spear, and with a shield: but I come to thee in the name of the Lord of hosts, the God of the armies of Israel, whom thou hast defied"*. The Apostle Paul knew the Jesus Christ he was preaching and the power of Jesus Christ, as for the seven sons of Sceva, they didn't know the Jesus Christ Paul was preaching, neither had they any knowledge of the power of this Jesus Christ Paul was preaching. *Acts 19:14-16 "And there were seven sons of one Sceva, a Jew and chief of the priests, which did so. 15And the evil spirit answered and said, Jesus I know, and Paul I know; but who are ye? 16And the man in whom the evil spirit was leaped on them, and overcame them, and prevailed against them, so that they fled out of that house naked and wounded"*. Take note, the evil spirits know God and the power of Jesus Christ, the evil spirits knew Paul, and also knew that Paul was filled with the power of God. Likewise, every Christian needs to know that he or she is well known by the devil and every demon in hell, so if you think you can escape this battle you are in, then, you must be deceiving yourself.

If there was no warfare for the Christian to fight, God would not have asked the Christian to put on the whole amour of God. Hell is daily intensifying its activities against the kingdom of heaven, Christians, and the rest of humanity in these last days. Christians that are dwelling in spiritual laziness these last days could be easy prey for the devil. The devil fully knows what he is after, therefore it is time for us Christians to get up and do what we are supposed to be doing. The children of God have for long been suffering violent attacks from the kingdom of darkness and therefore the Lord Jesus Christ said, only they violent will overcome. *Mathew 11:12 "And from the days of John the Baptist until now the kingdom of heaven suffereth violence, and the violent take it by force".* Spiritual violence by a Christian against the kingdom of darkness is not a sin before God. God's agenda is to raise spiritually violent Christians that will harass Satan and his demons and deliver the captives. So wake up and get onboard today.

Chapter 12

You must live a holy life.

Holiness, Holiness, Holiness; it is time for the church of God to realize that our God is a holy God. God dwells in absolute holiness, a symbol of God's absolute purity and righteousness. God is a holy God and that is what makes God unique. Holiness shows the sanctity of God's righteousness, purity and love. God's holiness shows the extent to which the judgment of God is just. God's holiness shows His unbiased nature and absolute absence of sin in God, and God's inability to compromise with sin. There is no sin in God, and God does not have the ability to compromise with sin. God's holiness reveals God's perfect nature; God makes no mistakes, therefore, no man is worthy of a "holiness" title.

Holiness also means perfection, to be holy is to be perfect in righteousness. "Living a holy life" is one of the requirements to enter heaven. *Hebrews 12:14 "Follow peace with all men, and holiness, without which no man shall see the Lord".* To be holy, is to live an absolutely righteous life; with no trace of sin. God requires everyman to live a holy life. Our Lord Jesus Christ said; "the prince of this world (Satan) cometh, but hath nothing in me". Jesus Christ was declaring that there is no sin in Him of which the devil can accuse Him. Holiness is God's nature and therefore anyone that desires to walk with God must live a holy life.

God first started telling mankind to be perfect (holy) in Genesis 17:1, when God appeared to Abraham. God dwells in glory and holiness, signifying the purity and beauty of God's glory. For any man to work with God, that man must live a holy life. Anything that is not holy is being defiled by sin and therefore God cannot put up with such things. God wants His children to live a life of holiness; "separation from sin and the world". Living a holy life is not working according to the flesh, but walking according to the leading of the Holy Spirit. *Romans 8:14 "For as many as are led by the Spirit of God, they are the sons of God".* Verse 1&2 *"There is therefore now no condemnation to them which are in Christ Jesus, who walk not after the flesh, but after the Spirit. ₂For the law of the Spirit of life in Christ Jesus hath made me free from the law of sin and death".* Verse 5-8 *"For they that are after the flesh do mind the things of the flesh; but they that are after the Spirit the things of the Spirit. ₆For to be carnally minded is death; but to be spiritually minded is life and peace. ₇Because the carnal mind is enmity against God: for it is not subject to the law of God, neither indeed can be. ₈So then they that are in the flesh cannot please God".* The following scriptures let us understand that; for any man or woman to truly walk with God, that man or woman must live/walk according to the leading of the Holy Spirit, and that anyone without the Holy Spirit of God does not belong to God.

Mankind is naturally born in sin and therefore entirely lacks the ability to naturally please God. *Psalm 51:5 "Behold, 1 was shapen in iniquity; and in sin did my mother conceive me". Romans 3:23 "For all have sinned and come short of the glory of God". 1 John 1:8 "If we say that we have no sin we deceive ourselves and the truth is not in us".* A life of holiness is a life lived according to the leading of the Holy Spirit of God, He teaches us to be righteous and to do the will of God. Remember, when God made man, mankind was perfect and in line with the will and purpose of God. But when Adam and Eve sinned, mankind loosed the perfection in which God created him. Now we can only get back the perfection in which God created us through the salvation the Lord Jesus Christ has brought us. So, living a holy life as a Christian cannot be achieved by yourself; it is the Holy Spirit of God dwelling in you that teaches you how to live a holy life (a life separated from sin).

We can only live a holy life when we walk according to the leading of the Holy Spirit living in us. This makes it clear that there is no way a person can please God without the Holy Spirit of God dwelling, leading, and working in that person. For us to function properly in our Christian walk, we need the Holy Spirit of God to dwell, teach, strengthen, and lead us into doing the will of God. *Philippians 2:13 "For it is God which worketh in you both to will and to do of His good pleasure". Leviticus 20:8(NIV) "Keep my decrees and follow them. I am the LORD, who makes you holy". 22:32(NIV) "Do not profane my holy name, for I must be acknowledged as holy by the Israelites. I am the LORD, who made you holy."*

It is the desire of God that everyone should be holy (perfect). *1 Peter 1:16 "for it is written: "Be holy, because I am holy." Mathew 5:48 "Be ye therefore perfect, even as your Father which is in heaven is perfect".* Because God is a holy God, He therefore requires that anyone that would dwell with Him in eternity should be holy. *Revelation 21:27(NIV) "Nothing impure will ever enter it, nor will anyone who does what is shameful or deceitful, but only those whose names are written in the Lamb's book of life."*

When God says "be holy", it is a command, not a plea. Without holiness no one will see God. God is holy and therefore requires all of His children to live a holy life. We can only be able to live a holy life when we allow the Holy Spirit of God to transform our lives. After receiving the Holy Spirit, the next step is transformation (sanctification). During this process, the spirit of God opens our understanding into knowing the will of God from sin, this knowledge backed by the fear of God in a person's life makes the person to love righteousness and hate sin; desiring righteousness and separating from sinful living. This clearly manifests in a person's life by making the person to be uncomfortable in any sinful situation. A true child of God would have no peace living in sin; that shows the fear of God and the presence of the Holy Spirit in someone's life. Only those that will live a holy life will see God.

Chapter 13

You must obey God's word.

Most people claim to be Christians, but they keep playing around God's word. One Clear way of distinguishing a true child of God from the multitude is; a true child of God fears God and therefore obeys God's word irrespective of the situation involved. Every word of God in the Bible is firm and sure and God cannot change it for anyone or for any reason, at any time.

Most Christians think that the Old Testament part of the Bible was only for the Jews and not for nowadays Christianity. This is a deception from the devil. God meant everything He said in His word, and there is nothing irrelevant in the Bible. From Genesis chapter 1 verse 1 to Revelation chapter 22 verse 21, God meant everything He said.

Some Christians think the Bible is mostly history; especially the Old Testament. This is not true; every event written in the Bible is true and did happened. *Ecclesiastes 1:9 "The thing that hath been, it is that which shall be; and that which is done is that which shall be done: and there is no new thing under the sun".* Those things were written for us to learn the good examples and practice them, and for us not to do the same mistakes that those people did. *Romans 15:4 "For whatsoever things were written aforetime were written for our learning, that we through patience and comfort of the scriptures might have hope". 1 Corinthians 10:11 "Now all these things happened unto them for ensamples: and they are written for our admonition, upon whom the ends of the world are come".*

There is nothing irrelevant in the Bible, and every word of God in the Bible is a command. God is not negotiating neither is He pleading with mankind to obey Him. God has set His standard and cannot change it. Do you think God sent His son Jesus Christ to die for nothing? Do not make that mistake; God does not have any favorites. Regardless of whomever you are in this life, or whatever you have attained in this life, God will not break His standard for your sake. Children and servants do not argue, only critics and opposition do argue. With God, those that obey His Commandments are those that love, honor, and please God. Those that do not obey God's commandments are those that hate God. *John 14:15 "If ye love me, keep my commandments". Verse 21 "He that hath my commandments, and keepeth them, he it is that loveth me: and he that loveth me shall be loved of my Father, and I will love him, and will manifest myself to him". Verses 23-24 "Jesus answered and said unto him, if a man loves me, he will keep my words: and my Father will love him, and we will come unto him, and make our abode with him. 24He that loveth me not keepeth not my sayings; and the word which ye hear is not mine, but the Father's which sent me". Matthew 7:21 "Not every one that saith unto me, Lord, Lord, shall enter into the kingdom of heaven; but he that doeth the will of my Father which is in heaven".*

This is God's standard for identifying a true Christian; a true Christian seeks to obey every word of God. A certain heresy preached in some churches today says; we are living in the period of grace and therefore God does not require our obedience. Men and women of faith that succeeded in their walked with God were obedient to God's word. A parent's love will continue to grow for a child that is obedient, and the opposite is true for a disobedient child. An obedient Child will bring honor to the parents, but a foolish and disobedient child will bring disgrace to the parent. *Proverbs 17:25 "A foolish son is a grief to his father, and bitterness to her that bare him"*. This is true between every believer and God. God calls us children; if we then are children to God, then we must obey God's word. It was obedience that caused Jesus Christ to leave heaven and come to this earth to die for the sins of mankind on the cross of cavalry. Jesus Christ honored his Father by agreeing to die on the cross so that humanity can be saved from sin and death.

Obedience is the basis upon which our salvation is laid. God commanded that all those that will believe in His son Jesus Christ will have eternal life; if you don't obey, you won't believe, and if you don't believe, you can't be saved. If you obey God's word to believe in Jesus Christ, then you will be saved; because you obeyed God's word to believe in Jesus Christ. If any man or woman is to please God, that man or woman must obey the word of God. A person's obedience to God's word is a clear indication that the person knows God and belongs to God. Disobeying is equal to a challenging, and challenging is equal to fighting. Obedience is equal to submission, and submission brings loyalty which in turn strengthens the bond of friendship and unity.

The Friendship between God and Abraham existed because Abraham believed in God and was obedient to God's word. When God told Abraham to sacrifice his son Isaac, Abraham obeyed and did not argue with God. This is the kind of obedience God requires from His children. Though Abraham loved his son Isaac so much, yet he chose to obey God's word. If we are to please God, we must obey His word. God still requires obedience from His children.

When we obey God, we make God feels proud of us. Job was obedient to God's word, therefore God boasted about Job to Satan. *Job 1:8 "And the Lord said unto Satan, hast thou considered my servant Job, that there is none like him in the earth, a perfect and an upright man, one that feareth God, and escheweth evil"?* Here we see Satan did not ask God about how His servant Job was doing; it was God Himself that told Satan about Job's obedience to Him because God was pleased and proud of Job. This shows that when we obey God's word, we bring joy unto God's heart, but when we disobey God's word, the opposite happens. Read through the Bible; each time Israel disobeyed God's word, they loosed the battle to their enemies, but when they obeyed God's word, God gave them victory over their enemies. This is also true in our days, if we are obedient to God's word, God will protect, defend, and keep us safe from the evil one. If we are to have the victory over Satan and his demons, then we must obey God's word.

Every of our obedience to God's word does have a reward. When we obey God's word, God loves, blesses, guides, defends and keeps us safe. Christians are meant to be warriors and our captain is Jesus Christ, the Lord of host. If we obey our captain, He will teach us how to fight and get the victory. *Psalm 144:1 "Blessed be the Lord my strength, which teacheth my hands to war and my fingers to fight".* The Apostle Paul said that a Christian should put on the whole amour of God in other to be able to withstand in the evil day. *Ephesians 6:13 "Wherefore take unto you the whole amour of God, that ye may be able to withstand in the evil day, and having done all, to stand".* Remember, the amour belongs to God, and it is clear that; "God will only allow those that obey His words to use His amour". We are living in the evil days mentioned in this verse. This shows how important it is for every Christian to obey every word of God.

Chapter 14

Know your enemy and know his tricks.

Knowing your enemy and knowing the strength and skills of your enemy, automatically puts you a step ahead to your victory. If you do not know the tricks of your enemy, the strength and skills that your enemy uses against you, then you are sure to be a victim at all times. It is very essential that a warrior knows the skills, and weapons, and strength of his enemy. If you lack this knowledge about your enemy, you will never have the victory.

When I was in high school, one of my teachers always said; "understanding the content of the question is part of the answer". That's a true saying. If you are asked a question, and you respond without understanding the content of the question, you end up giving a foolish response. So also every Christian needs to study the tricks of the devil, the strategies the devil uses against us. It is more dangerous to be ignorant of one's enemy than to surrender to that enemy. The apostle Paul warns us not to be ignorant of the devices/tricks of Satan and his demons. *2 Corinthians 2:11 "Lest Satan should get an advantage of us: for we are not ignorant of his devices".* Just as God requires every Christian to study His word (the Bible), likewise, it is required of every Christian to know the tricks of the devil. With all the power that God has made available for the Christian, not knowing the tricks of the devil is equal to not having any power at all. Simply knowing who your enemy is, is not enough, but knowing the strength and tricks of your enemy gets you closer to your victory.

One of the reasons why the church is not able to fully exercise God's power nowadays is because the church is ignorant of most of Satan's devices. Jesus Christ said He has given us power to trample and crush serpents and Scorpions and all the power of Satan and his demons. *Luke 10:19 "Behold, I give unto you power to tread on serpents and scorpions, and over all the power of the enemy: and nothing shall by any means hurt you".* Though Christians have the power to trample over every serpent and Scorpion and over all the power of Satan and his demons, yet if a Christian is ignorant of the devices/tricks of the serpents, Scorpions, Satan and his demons, that Christian is very likely to be the victim. Satan is a roaring lion, a very old and well experienced devil. Satan deceived Adam, so be careful and be wise; the devil is the most deceptive being.

When a Christian is ignorant of the devices of the devil, that very Christian opens the door for the enemy to enter and afflict him or her. *1 peter 5:8 "Be sober, be vigilant; because your adversary the devil, as a roaring lion, walketh about, seeking whom he may devour".* This verse lets us know that the devil cannot devour everyone. The devil is desperately looking for those that are ignorant of his devices so he can devour them. A Christian needs to be spiritually and physically sober and vigilant at all times. The careless ones become easy prey for Satan and his demons.

Ignorance and carelessness can cost a person everything including his or her very life. Fools die for their foolishness, likewise, the ignorant ones dies for their ignorance. Any Christian that lacks knowledge about the devices of Satan is likely to have Satan as his or her guest of honor. *2 Corinthians 11:14 "And no marvel; for Satan himself is transformed into an angel of light"*. It is only a fool that keeps repeating the same thing, and each time expecting a better result. Wise people on the other hand take different approaches. Therefore, they are most likely to achieve better results. New innovations are mostly products of a good research. So also to get an edge over Satan, a good research about Satan's tricks can mean a good payoff.

If only a Christian can give a good attention to the moves made by the devil, that Christian is most likely able to know when the devil is at work. The reason most Christians go through certain troubles these days is because of their ignorance of Satan's devices. God expects us to learn certain lessons out of every situation we go through; lessons learned from one situation should be a point of reference, and should serve as an example to us for overcoming subsequent situations we may face in the future. If Satan attacks you today from the East side, you should keep track of that for a future reference. This will help you to easily identify any future attack that Satan might launch on the East side again. Satan doesn't have new tricks; he is still using those old tricks he deceived Adam and Eve with, but he now applies them in different forms and approach.

Chapter 15

You must know the front you are battling from.

When a warrior understands the front on which he is fight, the fight becomes even easier for that warrior. Spiritual battles are fought spiritually. For the success of a Christian to manifest itself in the physical realm, it must first be achieved in the spiritual realm. The spiritual comes before the physical; the spiritual realm dominates the physical realm. For the Christian to succeed in this physical life, success must have been obtained and established first in the spiritual realm.

God our Creator is a spirit and therefore requires that anyone serving God should serve Him in spirit and in truth. *John 4:24 "God is a Spirit: and they that worship Him must worship Him in spirit and in truth".* This verse is telling us that God operates mainly in the spiritual realm, since God is a spirit. Because God is a spirit, the physical man cannot see God with his physical eyes. God made man a tree part being; man is mainly a spirit being, having a soul, and dwelling in a body. *1 Thessalonians 5:23 "And the very God of peace sanctify you wholly; and I pray God your whole spirit and soul and body be preserved blameless unto the coming of our Lord Jesus Christ".* God is a spirit and therefore created man to be a spirit being having a soul (will power) living in the flesh. The flesh is mere dust which God molded to shelter man's spirit and soul. This clearly shows that; the real you is not your flesh (physical structure), but your spirit. Therefore when a person dies; the body rots away, the spirit goes back to God, and the soul faces God's judgment. *Ecclesiastes 12:7 "Then shall the dust return to the earth as it was: and the spirit shall return unto God who gave it".* This becomes real when someone is dreaming. In your dream; your body lays down tired and is resting, but you recognized yourself involved in a different activity. When you wake up from your dream, you noticed that you actually did recognize yourself in your dream, and your dream occurs to you again like it was been recorded. This is what happens as you dream. During your dream; your body is tired and resting, totally unconscious. Whiles your spirit was you active in your dream, and your soul was the one that did record all the events of your dream and later brought it to your knowledge when you wake up, therefore you are able to remember all the events that took place in your dream.

Like God is a spirit, so also Satan and his demons are spirits. Humanity is basically caught in the middle of these two opposing spiritual forces. Satan, the enemy of the human soul is fighting humanity from a spiritual front. *Ephesians 6:12 "For we wrestle not against flesh and blood, but against principalities, against powers, against the rulers of the darkness of this world, against spiritual wickedness in high places". 2 Corinthians 10:3-4 "For though we walk in the flesh, we do not war after the flesh; for the weapons of our warfare are not carnal, but mighty through God to the pulling down of strong holds".* If a man or woman is to resist or war against the attacks of Satan upon his or her soul, then that man or woman needs to be born of the spirit of God (born-again). After a person confesses Jesus Christ as Lord and Savior and receives cleansing from his or her sins which automatically reconciles that person with God, Jesus Christ then baptizes that person with the Holy Spirit. To be baptized with the Holy Spirit is to be born of the Spirit (born-again). *John 3:3 "Jesus answered and said unto him, Verily, verily, 1 say unto thee, Except a man be born again, he cannot see the kingdom of God". Mathew 3:11 "1 indeed baptize you with water unto repentance: but he that cometh after me is mightier than I, whose shoes 1 am not worthy to bear: he shall baptize you with the Holy Ghost and with fire".* In verses 4-6 of John chapter 3, Nicodemus, a Jewish Rabbi, asked the Lord Jesus Christ this question; how can a man be born again? *"Nicodemus saith unto him, how can a man be born when he is old? Can he enter the second time into his mother's womb, and be born? 5"Jesus answered, Verily, verily, 1 say unto thee, except a man be born of water and of the Spirit, he cannot enter into the kingdom of God. 6 That which is born of the flesh is flesh; and that which is born of the Spirit is spirit".* As a person receives the baptism of the Holy Spirit, the Holy Spirit causes the spirit of that person to come alive. *John 6:63 "It is the spirit that quickeneth; the flesh profiteth nothing: the words that 1 speak unto you, they are spirit, and they are life".* The eyes of a person's spirit become opened as the person receives the baptism of the Holy Spirit; that makes a person to be able to understand spiritual things.

A sinner is one that is spiritually dead; the spirit of a sinner is dead and blind. Only God can bring that dead spirit of the sinner back to life through God' Spirit. This makes it impossible for anyone to serve God in the flesh. It is only when the spirit of a person comes alive then that person is able to serve God, because God the spirit. When a person is born of the Spirit, the person is able to communicate and fellowship with God. In order to communicate and fellowship with God, a person's spirit must be able to clearly hear and understand what God's Spirit is saying to him or her. For a person to truly serve God, that person's spirit must be alive and sound.

Warfare simply means war in the spiritual realm. Every true Christian is a notable enemy of Satan and his demons. When a person receives the baptism of the Holy Spirit, one of the physical signs is speaking in tongues. The Apostle Paul made us to understand that when a Christian prays in tongues, he or she is actually praying in the spirit; his or her spirit prays. As the believer prays in the spirit, he or she is warring in the spirit. *1 Corinthians 14:14 "For if 1 pray in an unknown tongue, my spirit prayeth, but my understanding is unfruitful".* This praying in tongues referred to by the Apostle Paul as "praying in an unknown tongue," is a spiritual language which the Holy Spirit of God grants unto a person's spirit after bringing that person's spirit alive.

Humanity is caught in the middle of a battle between two spirituality forces. Therefore, if a person is to stand against Satan and his devices, that person's spirit must be alive and sound. This can only be made possible through the intervention of God's Spirit in a person's life. When God created Adam in the Garden of Eden, God breathed into his nostrils the breath of life. *Genesis 2:7 "And the Lord God formed man of the dust of the ground, and breathed into his nostrils the breath of life; and man became a living soul"*. The breath of life that God breathed into Adam's nostrils became Adam's spirit, but when Adam sinned against God, Adam's spirit died (separated from God). And so because of sin, every individual is born into this world with his or her spirit separated from God. It is God's spirit in a person that makes the person to desire and walk in the nature and will of God, because the spirit God places in a person carries the nature of God and absolutely belongs to God. *Ecclesiastes 12:7 "Then shall the dust return to the earth as it was: and the spirit shall return unto God who gave it"*. So in other to please God, the spirit God placed in a man or woman must be reactivated (brought to life) again. Only the Holy Spirit of God can do this work in a person's life. So there in no way a man can please God or war against Satan and his demons without being baptized with the Holy Spirit of God. Since God is a spirit and God's call to every Christian is to walk with God in the Spirit, it should then be clear that every opposition and attack a Christian faces against God's call in his or her life is Spiritual and can only be resisted in the spiritual realm. Since Satan and his demons are spirits, it also means that Satan and his demons attack a Christian in the spirit. Therefore, if a Christian is to fight back against the attacks of Satan and his demons, then that Christian must fight back in the spirit which means that the battle front is in the spirit realm. *Ephesians 6:12(NLT) "For we are not fighting against flesh and blood enemies: but against evil rulers and authorities of the unseen world, against mighty powers in this dark world, and against evil spirits in the heavenly places"*.

Chapter 16

You must know how to pray warfare prayers.

One thing the Church needs to be aware of these last days is that; the days of ceremonialism and protocol in prayer have been over long since. These days, Christianity is meant for vigilant, sober and prayerful individuals. When our Lord Jesus Christ was still on earth with His twelve disciples, all twelve of the disciples used to sleep while the Lord was praying. When Jesus Christ used to tarry in prayer all night, Peter and the other twelve were slumbering. *Matthew 26:40 "Then He returned to the disciples and found them asleep; He said to Peter, couldn't you watch with me even one hour?"*

If any man or woman is to succeed in his or her walk with God these days, that man or woman must be able to pray. Peter and the other twelve disciples used to sleep when Jesus was praying, because at that time, the disciples had not received the baptism of the Holy Spirit yet. Until a man or woman is filled with the Holy Spirit, he or she cannot find the strength to pray. There is no record in the Bible indicating that our Lord Jesus Christ used to tarry in prayer before the day he was baptized by John the Baptist, and the Holy Spirit came upon Him. But immediately the Holy Spirit came upon Jesus Christ, the Bible records that; the Holy Spirit led Jesus Christ into the wilderness to fast and pray for forty days and forty nights. *Matthew 3:16 "After His baptism, as Jesus came up out of the water, the heavens were opened and He saw the Spirit of God descending like a dove and settling on Him". 4:1-2 "Then Jesus was led by the Spirit into the wilderness to be tempted there by the devil. ₂For forty days and forty nights He fasted and became very hungry".* When the Holy Spirit led Jesus Christ into the wilderness to fast for forty days and forty nights, Jesus Christ was not only fasting, but He also was praying. During His forty days and forty nights in the wilderness, our Lord Jesus Christ was involved in a spiritual warfare. It was after His forty days and forty nights fasting that the Lord Jesus Christ started His public ministry. This shows that as a Christian, we cannot operate in the supernatural without being filled with the Holy Spirit of God.

Before the day of Pentecost, the disciples were always sleeping while their master prayed. But then a sudden change came in the life of the slumbering disciples after they were baptized with the Holy Spirit on Pentecost. *Act 2:1-4 "On the day of Pentecost all the believers were meeting together in one place. ₂Suddenly, there was a sound from heaven like the roaring of a mighty windstorm, and it filled the house where they were sitting. ₃Then, what looked like flames or tongues of fire appeared and settled on each of them. ₄And everyone present was filled with the Holy Spirit and began speaking in other languages, as the Holy Spirit gave them this ability".* The dramatic event that took place on the day of Pentecost among the disciples: brought about an overwhelming change in the lives of all the disciples; that change led to the birth of the church. Immediately after the disciples received the baptism of the Holy Spirit on the day of Pentecost, they became known as men and women of prayer. Acts 6:4 "But we will give ourselves continually to prayer, and to the ministry of the word". Peter, the disciple notably identified for sleeping in Matthew 26:40; now became the man of prayer in Acts 6:4.

When the Lord Jesus Christ was teaching, His disciples asked Him to teach them how to pray. *Luke 11:1 "And it came to pass, that, as He was praying in a certain place, when He ceased, one of His disciples said unto Him, Lord, teach us to pray, as John also taught his disciples".* In response to that disciple's request, the Lord Jesus Christ taught them to pray 'the Lord's prayer'. Verse 2 - 4. That was all the disciples needed to Pray at that time. But then, when the Holy Spirit came upon the disciples on the day of Pentecost, the Bible recorded a change of pattern in prayer. Gentle prayers do not bother Satan and his demons any longer; ceremonial prayers do not move Satan and his demons any longer, neither is the kingdom of darkness hindered by lukewarm prayers any more. The only prayer that puts Satan and his demons to flight these days is a violent Holy Spirit inspired prayer. The cunningly gentle, crafty, and deceptive Serpent introduced in Genesis 3:1; has now become extremely arrogant and defiant against God's church and creation. The only language Satan and his demons understand these days is the language of violent prayer inspired by the Holy Spirit. *Matthew 11:12 "And from the days of John the Baptist until now, the kingdom of heaven suffereth violence, and the violent take it by force".* Satan and his demons are every day researching the kingdom of God and the church of Jesus Christ in other to develop new strategies against the people of God. Likewise, the church of Jesus Christ needs to become more spiritually violent and aggressive towards the kingdom of darkness if we are to succeed. To prove to you that Satan and his demons carry out researches in other to develop new strategies in their fight against Christians, we would look at *Psalm 91:11 "For he shall give his angels charge over thee, to keep thee in all thy ways".* Satan had long being casted out of heaven. Thousands of years later, the verse coated above in Psalm 91 was written. Now someone may ask; where did the devil get this same scripture of Psalm 91:11 that he used to tempt our Lord Jesus Christ in *Matthew 4:6 "And saith unto Him, If thou be the Son of God, cast thyself down, for it is written; He shall give His angels charge concerning thee: and in their hands they shall bear thee up, lest at any time thou dash thy foot against a stone".* It is clear that the devil was only able to know this Scripture in Psalm 91:11 because he devil went and read through the writings of Psalm 91 unknowingly to the author.

I see many churches around today that do pray with protocol and intelligence; folks don't want to get their bodies sweating as they pray. Satan is a mad dog, and a roaring lion with extreme arrogance against God and all of God's creation; Satan doesn't understand gentleness of any kind. The Bible recorded that, our Lord Jesus Christ; before going to the cross, prayed earnestly, and His sweat was turned into blood. If only through prayer, the Lord Jesus Christ was sweating, then it must be that the Lord Jesus Christ was praying violently. But it was not just the sweat; His sweat was as it were great drops of blood. This shows how angry Jesus Christ was in His spirit, and knowing all the pains and torture He was to go through on the cross for the sins of mankind, Jesus Christ became even more-angry in His spirit. *Luke 22:44 "And being in an agony; He prayed more earnestly and His sweat was as it were great drops of blood falling down to the ground".*

Gentleness against the kingdom of darkness would yield no results, only the violent can take their portion by force. Satan and his demons are more-wicked than anyone can imagine; those are demons that are more-wicked to the extent that even Satan does not have control over them. Therefore when confronting such personalities, the born-again Christian has to be spirituality violent. Do not dream of confronting these personalities when you have not received the Holy Spirit yet. To confront these evil personalities and take back your portion, deliver the captives, set the prisoners free, grant liberty to the oppressed, grant sight to the blind, heal the broken-hearted, and preach the good news to the poor; it is your sole responsibility as a born again Christian, because the Lord Jesus Christ has anointed you with the Holy Spirit. *Luke 4:18 "The Spirit of the Lord is upon me, because He hath anointed me to preach the gospel to the poor; He hath sent me to heal the brokenhearted, to preach deliverance to the captives, and recovering of sight to the blind, to set at liberty them that are bruised". Jeremiah 1:10 "See, I have this day set thee over the nations and over the kingdoms, to root out, and to pull down, and to destroy, and to throw down, to build, and to plant". Luke 10:19 "Behold, I give unto you power to tread on serpents and scorpions, and over all the power of the enemy: and nothing shall by any means hurt you".* In this 19th verse of Luke chapter 10, we are told that every born again Christian has been given the power of God to trample over all the power of the enemy, and our Lord Jesus Christ gave a guarantee too; that nothing shall by any means hurt His own (the born again Christian). As long as you are a born again Christian having the spirit of God in you, and you are not living in sin; God's Spirit is living in you and God's power has been made available to you. So rise up today and exercise your authority over the kingdom of darkness; having this confidence, that you have heaven's approval and God is on your side. *Romans 8:31 "What shall we then say to these things, if God be for us; who can be against us?"* If you are a born again Christians, you should not be fearful of the hosts of hell, because God whose power is supreme in the entire universe is standing with you and no dog will move its tongue against you. *Exodus 11:7 "But against any of the children of Israel shall not a dog move his tongue, against man or beast: that ye may know how that the Lord doth put a difference between the Egyptians and Israel".* Every Holy Spirit filled Christian is an Israelite spiritually, because of the spirit of adoption dwelling in us, and this is the difference that God has put between the Egyptians (the ungodly) and the Israelites (the children of God). So do not be afraid of the intimidations of Satan and his demons; be bold, for the Lord will not disappoint His own. *2 Timothy 1:7 "For God hath not given us the spirit of fear: but of power, and of love, and of a sound mind".*

Chapter 17

What if I do not fight my battles?

Every man and every woman born into this earth have a battle to fight. Everyone is naturally born into a battle. Identifying and locating the source of your battle at an early age, will contribute greatly towards your future success and greatness. *Lamentations 3:27 "It is good for a man that he bear the yoke in his youth".* Job said; "People are born for trouble as readily as sparks fly up from a fire". Job 5:7. The troubles of many people start from their conception. So by the time they are born into this world, their troubles are already at the stage of maturity. The Bible recorded that King Pharaoh ordered the midwives to kill any Hebrew boy that was to be born, because a deliverer was to be born who was to deliver the children of Israel from slavery in Egypt. *Exodus 1:15-16 "The king of Egypt said to the Hebrew midwives, whose names were Shiphrah and Puah, ₁₆When you are helping the Hebrew women during childbirth on the delivery stool, if you see that the baby is a boy, kill him; but if it is a girl, let her live."* King Pharaoh gave this decree in other to destroy Moses, who was to be the deliverer of the children of Israel from slavery even before Moses was born. In order to destroy one Moses, Pharaoh also commanded the Egyptians to throw every Hebrew boy into the Nile River. *Exodus 1:22 "Then Pharaoh gave this order to all his people: every Hebrew boy that is born you must throw into the Nile, but let every girl live."* Because Pharaoh wanted to destroy a single Hebrew boy that was prophesied to be the deliverer of the children of Israel from slavery in Egypt, Pharaoh ended up killing and destroying many other destinies. So the battle against Moses started long before Moses was finally giving birth to. This was just one aspect of the battles that were against Moses and his destiny.

The second battle that Moses had to face was the battle of a curse Jacob issued on two of his sons; Simeon and Levi, for killing Hamor, and his son Shechem, and the men of their city, because Shechem had sexually assaulted their sister Dinah. *Genesis 34:25-26 "And it came to pass on the third day, when they were sore, that two of the sons of Jacob, Simeon and Levi, Dinah's brethren, took each man his sword, and came upon the city boldly, and slew all the males. ₂₆And they slew Hamor and Shechem his son with the edge of the sword, and took Dinah out of Shechem's house, and went out".* Out of anger, Simeon and Levi, killed all the men of the city, not regarding the covenant their father Jacob had made with the people. Because of their actions, Jacob cursed Simeon and Levi before he died. *Genesis 49:5-7 "Simeon and Levi are brethren; instruments of cruelty are in their habitations. ₆O my soul, come not thou into their secret; unto their assembly, mine honor, be not thou united: for in their anger they slew a man, and in their self will they dig down a wall. ₇Cursed be their anger, for it was fierce; and their wrath, for it was cruel: I will divide them in Jacob, and scatter them in Israel".* Hundreds of years later after Jacob had placed a curse on Simeon and Levi for their anger, innocent Moses, was later born to a Levite father by a Levite mother. Meaning, Moses was now carrying a double package of the curse Jacob placed on Simeon and Levi because of their anger. *Lamentations 5:7 "Our fathers have sinned, and are not; and we have borne their iniquities".* Simeon and Levi acted wickedly and their father Jacob cursed them. Simeon and Levi died hundreds of years before innocent Moses was born. Moses walked with God very closely, God delivered the children of Israel from slavery through Moses, God demonstrated His power, signs and wonders, and great miracles through Moses. But at the very last moment, the anger for which Jacob had cursed Levi finally manifested itself in the life and ministry of Moses. Remember, Satan started fighting Moses before he was born, and continued fighting Moses throughout his life time and even fought over the man's corpse. *Jude verse 9ₐ "Yet Michael the archangel, when contending with the devil he disputed about the body of Moses".* Levi's anger was flowing in Moses' blood, and that anger finally caught up with Moses at the peak of his ministry. God commanded Moses to take the rod and speak to the rock, God did not tell Moses to strike the rock, but out of anger; Moses smote the rock, which was a clear disobedience to the command God gave him.

Also, for the purpose of a better understanding of this chapter, we shall look at the events that surrounded the birth, life, death and resurrection of our Lord Jesus Christ. Long before our Lord Jesus Christ was born, the devil had already raised up King Herod to destroy Jesus Christ. God had long revealed to the prophet Jeremiah, the evil plan of the devil to kill Jesus Christ hundreds of years before Jesus Christ was born. *Jeremiah 31:15 "Thus saith the Lord; a voice was heard in Ramah, lamentation, and bitter weeping; Rachel weeping for her children refused to be comforted for her children, because they were not".* When King Herod finally realized that he was being mocked by the three wise men, King Herod ordered that all the children age two and below should be killed. *Matthew 2:16 "Then Herod, when he saw that he was mocked of the wise men, was exceeding wroth, and sent forth, and slew all the children that were in Bethlehem, and in all the coasts thereof, from two years old and under, according to the time which he had diligently inquired of the wise men".* This clearly shows that; even before Jesus Christ was born, the devil had already put King Herod in position to kill Jesus Christ. Right through His ministry, the Bible tells us of different attacks on the life and ministry of Jesus Christ. During His ministry, many attempts were made to kill Jesus Christ, even before the appointed time. When the time finally came that Jesus Christ was to be crucified for the sins of mankind, the devil was still fighting Him. Even when Jesus Christ finally gave up the ghost on the cross and His body was laid in the tomb, the devil still wanted to ensure that Jesus Christ was truly dead and that no prophet sent by God will be able to access the corpse of Jesus Christ and raise Him up from the grave, that was why the devil organized guards to be on watch at the tomb. *Matthew 27:66(NLT) "So they sealed the tomb and posted guards to protect it".* What Satan failed to realize then was that; no physical army can stop the Holy Spirit from doing His work.

So then, the answer to the question is this; *if you do not fight your battles, your battles will come after you and fight you.* Even though he was highly anointed by God, yet the battle of Moses was still pursuing him. And because Moses did not pray (fight) and destroy the curse of anger that was issued on his ancestor Levi centuries before he was born, Moses finally had to pay a bitter prize.

Chapter 18

Success will be harder.

Have you ever wondered why success is the hardest of things for most people? It is obvious that a person's success would be directly proportional to the level of victory which that person has attained in the spiritual realms. This is mostly true for people who have come to be born again, but with generational spiritual yokes and bondages. Every true success and true riches come from God, and every believer should know that; the devil is not only fighting against your soul, but the devil is also fighting against your progress, your success, your achievements, your joy, your happiness, you peace and everything you lay your hands on to do. God is the creator of all things in the entire universe. Therefore, every gift that a man gets from God is original and perfect. *Psalms 24:1 "The earth is the Lord's, and the fullness thereof; the world, and they that dwell therein". Isaiah 66:2ₐ "For all those things hath mine hand made, and all those things have been, says the Lord". James 1:17 "Every good gift and every perfect gift is from above, and cometh down from the Father of lights, with whom is no variableness, neither shadow of turning".* Anything that is ever good in this earth originates from God. It is only God that can give a person true success, riches and prosperity. *Deuteronomy 8:18 "But thou shalt remember the Lord thy God: for it is He that giveth thee power to get wealth, that He may establish His covenant which He swore unto thy fathers, as it is this day".* Though a person might be rich and prosperous in this life, but if those riches and prosperity are not from God, then, God would not regard it, because those are not true riches and prosperity.

God created all things, and Satan created/creates nothing. It is only God that has created all things. There is nothing Satan has ever created in the history of his existence. What the devil does is this: the devil snatches away the good gifts God gives to His children and pretends to be the owner of those gifts, and that is what the devil gives to those that seek the devil for wealth and prosperity, but the truth is; every gift the devil gives to a person, it is in turn for that person's soul.

When our Lord Jesus Christ was on earth, He said; when He ascends into heaven, He will give gifts unto men. *Ephesians 4:8 "Wherefore He saith, when He ascended up on high, He led captivity captive, and gave gifts unto men".* Heaven immediately grants every child of God under the covenanted blood of Jesus Christ anything they ask in the name of Jesus Christ according to the will of God. *John 14:13-14 "And whatsoever ye shall ask in my name, that will I do, that the Father may be glorified in the Son. ₁₄If ye shall ask any thing in my name, I will do it"*. God is eagerly waiting for His children to ask Him. For the eyes and ears of God are widely opened at all times to attend to the needs of His beloved children. Have you noticed a suckling mother? A suckling mother is always paying close attention to her baby in other to identify the needs of her baby, so she can give to her baby whatever her baby wants and is good for her baby. God also cares for the needs of His children in like manner. *Isaiah 49:15 "Can a woman forget her sucking child, that she should not have compassion on the son of her womb? Yea, they may forget, yet will I not forget thee"*.

What happens to many Christians, is this; when most Christians ask God for something and do not get or see the answer to their requests immediately: some lose faith, others forget about it, and others conclude; God doesn't want give me. That is not true, God always grant His children every request made in the name of Jesus Christ, as long as the request is in line with the will of God. But because God is a spirit and operates in the spirit, when a person asks God for anything, God releases the answer in the spirit realm and it sometimes take a while before it finally manifests in the physical. During this process, the devil attacks the blessing God has released for a person, and when that person is not consistent in praying for the blessing, the devil snatches it away. When Daniel made his request unto God for an understanding into the vision, God gave an answer to Daniel's request that same day, but the Prince of Persia resisted the manifestation of Daniel's request for 21 days. *Daniel 10:12-14 "Then said he unto me, fear not, Daniel, for from the first day that thou didst set thine heart to understand and to chasten thyself before thy God, thy words were heard, and I am come for thy words. ₁₃But the prince of the kingdom of Persia withstood me one and twenty days: but, lo, Michael, one of the chief princes, came to help me; and I remained there with the kings of Persia. ₁₄Now I am come to make thee understand what shall befall thy people in the latter days: for yet the vision is for many days"*. So likewise, there are forces of darkness resisting the manifestation of the blessings and gifts of many Christians today. If a Christian fail to deal with these forces of darkness through prayer and fasting, success can be even harder. Had it not been that Daniel tarried in prayer and fasting, he would not have received the answer to his request. This shows that God responds to every need of His children immediately. The reason why most times Christians don't get their blessings is because of this reason; the devil resists our blessings in the spirit realm, and when we are not effective in prayer to deliver our gifts and blessings from the attacks of the devil, we lose it.

Sometime ago, I was facing a situation of this nature. I needed a job desperately, because the job I was doing can barely pay my bills and get me some food. I was almost every day putting in applications for another job, but to no avail. In a month, I put in 20 to 30 applications, but not a call did I get from any of those employers. I started getting frustrated and was thinking God doesn't want to give me a job. I began to question myself; am I in the will of God? Is it that I have sinned? Is there something God wants me to do which I am not doing? And those were the times when a friend will come and tell me of the new job he just got, or the good paying job for which he was interviewed last week. And this will add up to my frustrations and make me ask more questions. Not until one day I set my heart to fast and pray seriously. In a week, I saw a tremendous change. On average since then, for every five application I send out, I get a call or two from employers. Since then, getting a job has not been any difficult for me.

Chapter 19

Living a Pure and a Holy Christian life will be more difficult.

It is very true that once saved is not forever saved. A person can be save, but if there are bondages and yokes still in place in that person's life, he or she can find it very difficult to serve and please God. Foundational and generational powers are responsible for most of the frustrations many Christians are facing today in their walk with God. It is very clear that God doesn't call a person to Himself in other to frustrate that person. What limits most Christians in their walk and fellowship with God is directly connected to the bondages and yokes attached to their generation and foundation. The devil might not be able to stop a person from confessing Jesus Christ as Lord and receiving salvation, but the devil will put hindrances of every kind to limit that person from reaching the heights to which God has called him or her. The devil might not to be able to stop you from walking with God, but the devil will ensure that for every step of your way in walking with God, there are pot holes to make you slip and fall. That is why it is good for a man to face and conquer the battles in his or her life after accepting Jesus Christ and been baptized with the Holy Spirit. Though a person may be born again, but if those foundational and generational bandages and yokes remain in place, that person can serve and worship the God of peace all his life but will never enjoy the peace of God.

Moses probably learned about the curse Jacob placed upon his ancestor Levi, for killing in revenge to the defilement of his sister, Dinah. Had Moses prayed and cancelled the curse Jacob issued on Simeon and Levi, his feet would have tread on the promise land for which he suffered so much. If it were not for God's mercy, Moses would have missed heaven. Throughout Moses' ministry, Jacob's curse was still flowing from one generation to the other. The anointing upon Moses' life did not prevent Moses from meeting up with the bitter outburst of anger that was flowing in his foundation.

One of the Bible Character that knew his foundation was faulty was, Jabez. *1 Chronicles 4:9-10 "Jabez was more honorable than his brothers. His mother had named him Jabez, saying, I gave birth to him in pain."* ₁₀Jabez cried out to the God of Israel, Oh, that you would bless me and enlarge my territory! Let your hand be with me, and keep me from harm so that I will be free from pain. And God granted his request". From Genesis to Revelation, Jabez appeared only in two verses of 1 chronicles chapter 4. Jabez mother did not only bare him in pain, but Jabez was also very poor. Jabez had to take his situation unto God in prayer, asking for God's intervention his life. Before Jabez could arrive into the world, he was already facing trouble. The day Jabez finally realized there was a rage of poverty against him and his family, Jabez cried out to the God of Israel for help. It is very clear that; had Jabez not call on the God of Israel, Jabez would have died a pauper.

Samson was a man highly anointed by God, but Samson had a problem of immorality in his foundation. When the angel of God appeared and declared the purpose of God for the child that was to be born, Manoah and his wife obeyed everything that the angel of God had said to them. *Judges 13:3-5 "The angel of the LORD appeared to her and said, you are barren and childless, but you are going to become pregnant and give birth to a son. ₄Now see to it that you drink no wine or other fermented drink and that you do not eat anything unclean. ₅You will become pregnant and have a son whose head is never to be touched by a razor because the boy is to be a Nazirite, dedicated to God from the womb. He will take the lead in delivering Israel from the hands of the Philistines."* Samson's parents obeyed the words of the angel of God that had appeared to them, and Samson's mother never drank wine or any other fermented drink during her time of pregnancy, neither did Samson's parents use any razor on his head. Though Samson's parents strictly warned him about God's purpose in his life and that he was never to allow the secret of his strength to be known. Despite all the warnings his parents had given him, Samson refused to listen to his parents and was going after prostitutes. *Judges 16:1" One day Samson went to the Philistine town of Gaza and spent the night with a prostitute".* Had Samson identified his problem of immorality and prayed for God to deliver him, he would not have found himself on the laps of Delilah. Samson, a man highly anointed by God, ended his life and ministry as prisoner of war and a laughingstock for children of slaves.

The reason why you see many people today who started walking with God in a very healthy spiritual manner later on turn out to be backsliders after a few years is because of the generational and foundational battles raging against them. When these powers are in operation against a person's life, living a healthy Christian life can be very difficult and burdensome. I knew a born again sister who came to know the Lord a few years before I did. A sister well devoted and committed to the things of God. This sister had been a born again over two years before I came to know her. She was in the choir group and was always in the church facility cleaning and dressing the sanctuary. During one of the monthly deliverance services, a serpentine spirit manifested in the sister as prayer was going on. The serpentine spirit in the sister was claiming that he is a king and that the sister belongs to him. The pastor asked the spirit; why do you say this sister belongs to you? And the spirit spoke through the sister in a manly voice, saying; many years ago, the father of this lady had asked this demonic personality for riches and fame with an agreement that he will give his two young daughters in marriage to the demonic personality. The father of the sister became rich in no time and had fame as well. Years after her father died, the innocent sister got married and became a born again Christian not knowing the covenant her father had entered into. And though the sister loved God and was determined to pursue righteousness, holiness and purity in her walk with God, yet she was finding it difficult in her Christian life and in her marriage life. This evil personality had been fighting and causing frustrations for this sister on every side, since the day she got married and came to know the Lord. Even after she had become a born again

Christian, the covenant her father made by giving her and her elder sister in marriage to the serpentine spirit in exchange for riches and fame was still affecting her life seriously. This sister ended up leaving the Fellowship and the frustrations caused her husband who was the keyboardist to also leave the Fellowship. This shows the extent to which the bondages and yokes in a person's lineage and foundation can hinder him from walking with God if they are not thoroughly addressed in prayer.

Chapter 20

It can cost a person eternal life

The thoughts and wishes of Satan and his demons for every person living on this earth; is to lead that person into the everlasting fires of hell. Every move and every attack of the devil against any man or woman is geared towards the damnation of that person's Soul. The devil is always targeting the weak areas in the lives of men and women in other to bring them down in a moment. The higher the height of a person's walk with God, the more the kingdom of darkness intensifies its activities against that person. Unbelievers are mostly not an effective target of the devil, but true believers in Jesus Christ, are always an effective target of the devil and his demons, at all times.

Moses was born into a serious battle. From childhood, the enemy had already made arrangements for his elimination before he could reach his first birthday. *Exodus 1:22 "And Pharaoh charged all his people, saying; every son that is born ye shall cast into the river, and every daughter ye shall save alive"*. Though the devil failed to hinder the destiny of Moses at birth, yet the devil did not relent in his attacks against Moses, his destiny, and his soul. The devil ensured that the anger of Levi, the ancestor of Moses, manifested in Moses's ministry. *Genesis 49:5-7 "Simeon and Levi are brethren; instruments of cruelty are in their habitations. ₆O my soul, come not thou into their secret; unto their assembly, mine honor, be not thou united: for in their anger they slew a man, and in their self-will they dig down a wall. ₇Cursed be their anger, for it was fierce; and their wrath, for it was cruel: I will divide them in Jacob, and scatter them in Israel"*. The devil was not only fighting to destroy Moses' destiny, but was also pursuing Moses in other to destroy his soul in hell. Although the devil succeeded in causing Moses to disobey God's command out of anger, yet the devil was not satisfied, but went ahead to claim ownership over the corpse of Moses. *Jude 9 "Yet Michael the archangel, when contending with the devil he disputed about the body of Moses, durst not bring against him a railing accusation, but said, the Lord rebuke thee"*. The devil is not just trying to waste or destroy destinies, but he is also fighting to get the souls of men and women into eternal destruction.

Had it not been for the mercy of God, Samson would not have just perished in the hands of the Philistines, but would have also missed eternity with God. Because Samson failed to identify and deal with the passions of his flesh, therefore the devil then used Samson's weakness to fight against his ministry and his soul. *Judges 16:1*

"Then went Samson to Gaza, and saw there a harlot, and went in unto her". Samson had a serious problem with the sin of immorality in his life; lusting after strange women. Had it been that Samson realized earlier his weakness to control the desires of his flesh and ask God for deliverance, Samson would not have found himself sleeping on the devouring laps of Delilah. *Judges 16:19 "And she made him sleep upon her knees: and she called for a man, and she caused him to shave off the seven locks of his head; and she began to afflict him, and his strength went from him"*. Samson was smart to find: out death was creeping close to him after killing a thousand philistines with the jaw bone of an ass. *Judges 15:18-19 "And he was sore athirst, and called on the Lord, and said, thou hast given this great deliverance into the hand of thy servant: and now shall I die for thirst, and fall into the hand of the uncircumcised? 19But God clave a hollow place that was in the jaw, and there came water there out; and when he had drunk, his spirit came again, and he revived: wherefore he called the name thereof Enhakkore, which is in Lehi unto this day"*. When Samson became thirsty after killing the philistines, he knew he would have died of thirst. Samson called unto God, and God heard him instantly. And God caused water to flow out of the jawbone for Samson to drink. In like manner, if Samson had been smart enough to identify his weakness to bring under control the passions of his flesh, and call unto the same Lord he had called unto when he was dying of thirst, I believe God would have given him the strength to subdue his flesh. The weaknesses of our lives that we fail to identify and seek God's deliverance through prayer and fasting, will then become Satan's most effective weapon against us. Whether Samson was aware of the sin of immorality in his life or not, or he was aware of his weakness in subduing the passions of his flesh but ignored dealing with his weakness. The truth is; Samson paid a bitter prize, and that almost cost him eternal life. The anointing upon your life will not stop the devil from using your weaknesses to bring you down. When a mam fails to identify the weaknesses of his life and deal with them, the devil will then identify those witnesses and used them against that man. Unlike Samson who repeatedly involved himself in the sin of immorality and did not realize his weakness in time, King David was smart enough to immediately identify the sin of immorality as a weakness in his life, after his encounter with Uriah's wife. *2 Samuel 12:13a "And David said unto Nathan, I have sinned against the Lord"*.

Identify your weaknesses in time, and ask God for strength to overcome them. If you can't identify your weaknesses, ask the Spirit of God to search you and reveal your weaknesses unto you. Also ask the Holy Spirit to help you overcome them; this will help you greatly in living a victorious life and in your walk with God.